AROUND BERLIN IN 80 BEERS

PETER SUTCLIFFE

Cogan&Mater

Contents

Key to symbols

0 Place number
🍽 Food
U U-Bahn
S S-Bahn
H Tram
BUS Bus
⊗ Closed
🕐 Opening times
🍺 Boozer/unspoilt tavern
🍺 Brewery/brewpub
✕ Restaurant
✿ Garden/terrace
🏪 Shop
♫ Live music/performance
🛏 Accommodation
🚬 Indoor smoking area

Published by Cogan & Mater Limited.

© Cogan & Mater Limited 2011.
Managing Editor: Tim Webb.

First Published 2011.

Printed in the United Kingdom by Lavenham Press, Lavenham, Suffolk.

Design/typography: Dale Tomlinson
Typeface: FFUnit
Maps: OptaDesign

ISBN 978-0-9547789-8-9

Acknowledgements
To my long-suffering partner Pauline Doyle for expending much shoe leather in research and displaying the patience of a saint when I fouled-up our laptop; to my good friend Belgian beer maestro Stephen D'Arcy for teaching me how to distinguish a really special beer from one that is merely good; and to Germanophile and Bridge team captain Mike McHugh, who introduced me to some of the pubs in this guide and corrected my manuscript.

Picture credits
Some of the photographs in the opening sections of this book are by Berlin-based photographer and hotel manager **Paul Scraton**; the others are by the author and Pauline Doyle.

Around Berlin in 80 Beers has not accepted advertising or received any other form of payment or deal from any of the beer outlets featured in its pages. All entries were chosen entirely on their merits.

*...to the most vibrant and seductive city in Europe –
a place where history happens – and one of the
world's best places for drinking beer.*

Eighty years after Sally Bowles sang in cabaret and half a century after John F Kennedy declared himself a Berliner, Germany's capital city has reinvented itself to offer history, culture and entertainment in abundance ... and more great pubs than almost anywhere else.

Good pubs with great beer have always thrived here but since reunification re-established Berlin as the national seat of government, an influx of migrants from all over Germany has seen the arrival of regional pubs that showcase the beers, food and traditions of different regions.

The recent flowering of brewpubs, most of which make excellent and interesting beers, reflects a promising national trend that has seen the number of breweries in the country hold steady and now start to rise. The resumption of brewing at the old Kindl brewery in Neukölln bodes well too, though not everything in the Berlin beer garden is rosy.

In the late 19th Century Berlin had two hundred breweries, while today it has just fifteen, most of which are recent creations.

Although many Germans remain convinced they have both the most and the best brewers, producing the finest beer in the world, in truth the German brewing industry is under threat from declining consumption, the perpetual risk of takeover by global predators and a new threat, the very different approach to craft quality brewing that is impressing beer drinkers in the rest of the world.

Despite the central position of Bier in their national psyche, Germans drink far less of it than they did. In 1991, annual consumption per capita was 142 litres, the highest in Europe; by 2011 this has dropped to 110 – behind Ireland, the Czech Republic and even Austria.

Additionally, the simple but perfectly created brews that have for centuries been the backbone of German brewing have yet to impact on the growing global trade in top quality beer.

The world's four largest brewers (AB InBev, Heineken, SAB Miller and Carlsberg) hold between them only 20% of the German market, their products often dismissed as *Spülwasser* ("waste water"). German companies still dominate but small margins and declining sales have driven many to close, or else join large brewing groups in which rationalisation brings closure, amalgamation and the promotion of easy-to-make beers, all of which make them easier meat for a global player.

Privately owned bars often depend on generous start-up loans from large companies that tie them into selling duller, cheaper brands – tilting an already slippery slope.

Our aim in this book is to point younger Berliners and visitors alike to the sort of bars that have made Berlin one of the great experiences on the world tour of beer.

If all the pubs we feature are still going in five years time our endeavours will have been worthwhile.

Prost!

PETER SUTCLIFFE

3

Listings

Brewpubs

⑪ Brauhaus Bohnsdorf
⑫ Brauhaus Mitte
⑭ Brauhaus in Spandau
⑯ Brewbaker
㉓ Eschenbräu
㉙ Georgbräu
㊱ Hops & Barley
㊶ Lemke am Hackescher Markt
㊷ Lemke am Schloß
㊺ Lindenbräu
㊻ Marcus Bräu
(63) Schalander
(65) Schlossplatzbrauerei
(72) Südstern

Restaurants

(or Bars with full food menu)

❷ Alois S
❺ Alt-Berliner Weissbierstube
❻ Augustiner am Gendarmenmarkt
❽ Berliner Republik
⑪ Brauhaus Bohnsdorf
⑫ Brauhaus Mitte
⑬ Brauhaus in Rixdorf
⑭ Brauhaus in Spandau
⑮ Bräustübl
⑯ Brewbaker
⑲ Deponie #3
⑳ Dicke Wirtin
㉒ Endhorn
㉖ Gambrinus
㉗ Gasthaus Lentz
㉘ Gasthaus Wilhelm Hoeck 1892
㉙ Georgbräu
㉚ Glühwurm
㉝ Hax'nhaus
㉞ Hell oder Dunkel
㉟ Hopfingerbräu
㊲ zur Kleinen Markthalle
㊴ Latichte (Altberliner Schnappshaus)
㊵ zum Liebartz
㊶ Lemke am Hackescher Markt
㊷ Lemke am Schloß
㊸ zur Letzten Instanz
㊺ Lindenbräu
㊻ Marcus Bräu
㊼ Maria & Josef
㊽ Max und Moritz
㊾ Metzer Eck
㊿ Mittmann's
(51) Mommsen-Eck (Haus der 100 Biere)
(52) Mommseneck am Potsdamer Platz
(53) Mutter Hoppe
(54) zum Nußbaum
(56) zum Paddenwirt
(57) Paulaner's im Spreebogen
(58) Prater Garten & Gaststätte
(61) Restauration zur Gardestube
(63) Schalander
(64) Schillerklause
(68) zum Schusterjungen
(69) Schwarzwaldstuben
(70) Sophie'n Eck
(71) Strassenbahn
(72) Südstern
(73) Thüringer Stuben
(74) Tiergartenquelle
(75) Weihenstephaner
(76) Weisse Villa
(79) Yorckschlösschen
(80) Zillemarkt

BEER GARDEN OR OUTDOOR SEATING

1. Alkopole Bierbar
2. Alois S
5. Alt-Berliner Weissbierstube
6. Augustiner am Gendarmenmarkt
8. Berliner Republik
11. Brauhaus Bohnsdorf
12. Brauhaus Mitte
13. Brauhaus in Rixdorf
14. Brauhaus in Spandau
15. Bräustübl
16. Brewbaker
18. Clash
19. Deponie #3
22. Endhorn
23. Eschenbräu
26. Gambrinus
27. Gasthaus Lentz
29. Georgbräu
30. Glühwurm
31. Gottlob
33. Hax'nhaus
34. Hell oder Dunkel
35. Hopfingerbräu
36. Hops & Barley
37. zur Kleinen Markthalle
39. Latichte (Altberliner Schnappshaus)
41. Lemke am Hackescher Markt
42. Lemke am Schloß
45. Lindenbräu
47. Maria & Josef
49. Metzer Eck
51. Mommsen-Eck (Haus der 100 Biere)
52. Mommseneck am Potsdamer Platz
53. Mutter Hoppe
54. zum Nußbaum
56. zum Paddenwirt
57. Paulaner's im Spreebogen
58. Prater Garten & Gaststätte
63. Schalander
65. Schlossplatzbrauerei
71. Strassenbahn
72. Südstern
75. Weihenstephaner
76. Weisse Villa
79. Yorckschlösschen
80. Zillemarkt

LIVE MUSIC OR THEATRE

4. Ambrosius Bier Club
18. Clash
21. Dicker Wirt
48. Max und Moritz
53. Mutter Hoppe
55. Oberbaumeck or O.B.E.
71. Strassenbahn
72. Südstern
79. Yorckschlösschen

HOTEL OR ROOMS TO LET

14. Brauhaus in Spandau
35. Hops & Barley
48. Max und Moritz

SHOP

9. Bier Spezialitäten-Laden

BOOZERS/UNSPOILT TAVERNS

1. Alkopole
3. Alte Kolkschenke
4. Ambrosius Bier Club
5. Alt-Berliner Weissbierstube
7. Bechereck
10. Bornholmer Hütte
15. Bräustubl
17. Brink's
19. Deponie #3
20. Dicke Wirtin
21. Dicker Wirt
24. Felsenkeller
25. Gambrinus
27. Gasthaus Wilhelm Hoeck 1892
31. Hackbarth
33. Hell oder Dunkel
35. Hops & Barley
36. zur Kleinen Markthalle
37. Lange Nacht
38. Latichte
39. zum Liebartz
42. zur Letzen Instanz
43. Leuchturm
45. Marcus Bräu
47. Max und Moritz
48. Metzer Eck
49. Mittmann's
52. Mutter Hoppe
53. zum Nußbaum
54. Oberbaumeck
58. Quell Eck
59. zur Quelle
60. Restauration zur Gardestube
61. Reuterstuben
63. Schillerklause
66. Schnelle Quelle
67. zur Schusterjungen
69. Sophie'n Eck
70. Strassenbahn
74. Vogt's Bier Express
77. Westend Klause
78. Willy Bresch
79. Yorckschlosschen

Berlin is no beauty.

Unlike Prague, San Francisco or Edinburgh, there are few natural features to break up its unremitting flatness. Rather, it is raw and tough, shaped by determination and hard work. No other capital has risen so high and fallen so low over time, or so rarely been at ease with itself along its extraordinary journey.

Visiting in the 19th Century, the French writer Stendhal asked, "What could have possessed people to found a city amongst all this sand?" Goethe simply found the city "crude". Yet Berlin has its often turbulent history oozing from every pore.

The Prussians

In the 12th Century Berlin was no more than a remote trading post on the River Spree, ruled by a governor, or *Schultheiss*. In time its destiny became tied to that of the ambitious *Hohenzollern* dynasty, who from 1411 ruled Prussia for five centuries.

Berlin suffered more than most throughout the Middle Ages, with famines, the Black Death and the Thirty Years War, which ended in 1648. It only emerged from the shadows when the Great Elector, Friederick William, took the Prussian throne in 1640. He made peace with the Swedes, who were occupying Berlin, and established the city as the Prussian capital, creating

a web of authority, militarism and religious tolerance that (with the odd hiccup), became trademarks of Berlin.

His great-grandson, Frederick the Great, expanded Prussia by force and commissioned many spectacular Baroque monuments, mainly to himself, most of which survive.

The city's rollercoaster ride continued to go up – victory in the Seven Years War in 1763 – and down – defeat by Napoleon in 1806. Indeed when Bonaparte visited Frederick the Great's tomb in Potsdam, he is said to have remarked that, "If he were still alive, we would not be here."

Berlin rose again after Napoleon's defeat in 1815 at Waterloo, where perhaps appropriately it was the late arrival of Marshall Blücher's Prussian troops that proved decisive.

The Old Prussian Armoury – now the 'Museum of German History' – in Unter den Linden

The liberal revolutions that swept across Europe in 1848 failed to make a lasting impact. Instead, German unification was forged by Prussian *Eisen und Blüt* ('Iron and blood'). Prussian Chancellor Otto von Bismarck built on a series of strategically useful wars to unite all the various statelets and principalities of modern Germany to form the Second Reich in 1871. (For proportion, the First Reich was held to be the Holy Roman Empire.)

Capital of a united Germany

As the capital of a new nation, Berlin became an industrial powerhouse and the wealthy centre of a global empire, its population rocketing from 170,000 in 1800 to 4,000,000 by 1900.

This heyday did not last long, being destroyed by an economic disaster caused by the military stalemate of the 1914–18 War, in which 350,000 Berliners perished at the front and thousands more from malnutrition and cold as food and fuel supplies were diverted to the war effort.

Following the Armistice of November 1918, Berliners turned on their authorities and each other. Anger at four years of suffering and hardship was followed by several more of economic upheaval, endless civil strife and hyperinflation. At one stage in 1923, an entire wheelbarrow of *Reichsmark* banknotes could not buy a loaf of bread.

The short-lived Weimar Republic (1920–1933) brought an extraordinary burst of creativity. Kandinsky, Munch, Fritz Lang, Marlene Dietrich, Berthold Brecht and Kurt Weil were all here. This was the Berlin of Christopher Isherwood's *Sally Bowles*, later internationalised to a younger audience through the musical and film, *Cabaret*.

The rising menace

Berlin's lasting reputation has been for left-leaning politics. It was a Social Democratic stronghold as early as 1890. By the 1920s a powerful Communist presence had emerged. To break this stranglehold, Hitler sent Dr Joseph Goebbels to organise the ramshackle Nazi forces, something he achieved with characteristic flair.

Weimar was destined to be short-lived as conflicts between left and right turned the streets into a battleground. The Nazis under Adolf Hitler emerged victorious, and the great talents fled or were murdered.

It was more national than local support that propelled Hitler into power in 1933, though most Berliners eventually embraced the cause and cheered the early victories of the 1939–45 War.

Hitler had grandiose plans to remodel Berlin on a vast scale as 'Germania', the centrepiece of a Third Reich that would last for a thousand years. In time this vision, along with much of the city, was reduced to ashes by intensive allied bombing and in 1945 the Battle of Berlin.

'Grieving Parents'
by Käthe Kollwitz

The post-War carve-up

Time began again at *Stunde Null* – Zero Hour.

Berlin was divided into four occupation zones. Those run by the US, UK and France combined in 1948 to form West Berlin, while the Soviet sector became East Berlin, a capital for what in 1949 became the Deutsche Demokratische Republik (DDR), known in the west as East Germany.

The two halves of the city were rebuilt in contrasting styles. The East was utilitarian and Stalinist, the West modernist and functional. The border became the front line of the Cold War between the Communist and Capitalist worlds. For fifteen years, beginning with the blockade of 1948–49, Berlin was the epicentre of global politics in which numerous incidents almost sparked a third World War.

A barbed wire fence was constructed between the two Germanies in the early 1950s but the West Berlin loophole remained – the chink in Stalin's Iron Curtain. Around three and a half million East Germans, 20% of the population with a bias towards the intelligentsia, voted with their feet and fled to the West.

The DDR could not tolerate such an exodus indefinitely and at midnight on 13th August 1961 began construction of a 155 kilometre long wall encircling West Berlin cutting it off from the Russian sector and the rest of Germany.

For the West, the Berlin Wall came to represent all that was monstrous and inhuman about the Soviet system. The popular jibe was that it the only prison in the world where the prisoners lay outside the wall.

Ugly as it was though, the Wall created a situation that both sides could live with. Tension eased and the Cold War moved on and out of Europe to different battlefields, in Cuba, Africa and Vietnam.

Years of isolation

While Berlin became less important politically, West Berlin became a shop front for western values, democracy and conspicuous consumption.

However, largely cut off from mainstream Germany the enclave also became provincial in its ways. Heavily subsidised by the federal government and benefiting from a law that exempted its young men from military service it once more attained a certain Bohemian status, though isolation also brought severe social and economic problems in its wake.

East Berlin meanwhile also became a showcase, for socialist prestige projects. One in four employees worked for the state, and the city became 'Stasiville', where it seemed as if half the population were being rewarded for spying on each other and the other half.

The suburb of Karlshorst became home to the half-million strong Soviet Western Group of Forces, which along with its Warsaw Pact allies stood permanently poised to overrun Western Europe. But the real enemy came from within.

By the late 1980s, the DDR was on its knees economically. The fall of the Wall became inevitable but nonetheless still came as a shock when on 9th November

Bernauer Strasse in 1983

The Wall Breached – Potsdamer Platz in November 1989

1989, young men took lump hammers to it, broadcast live on hundreds of new channels around the world. In less than a year, re-unification had become a reality.

East Berliners flooded west, each armed with 100 Deutschmarks in 'welcome money'. Many seemed to buy bananas and not much else.

Modern day Berlin

Today, Berlin is capital of a reunified Germany. Since 1990 a frenzy of building and restoration work has transformed the centre. Where once Alsatian dogs and border guards patrolled the death-strip behind the Wall, a gleaming government and commercial quarter has emerged.

Restored tenements house media, fashion and internet businesses, along with smart shops and restaurants in a miraculous transformation. But the new urban chic still contrasts sharply with other districts where poverty and unemployment are as bad as anywhere in Europe, and where factory closures have left a population dependent on welfare.

Despite money flowing in since reunification, Berlin is poorer than the country it governs, with a per capita GDP barely half that of Hamburg. Unemployment is twice the national average and two-thirds of ex-East Germans (or *Ossis*) think they are treated like second-

class citizens. They resent the rich outsiders who transform their inner-city neighbourhoods into urban chic playgrounds. The physical divisions have gone, but a spiritual Wall remains.

In many former East Berlin suberbs, there is talk of *ostalgia* – a longing for the days of subsidy and security.

Has capital status been a curse? In 1900 Berlin was glorious and rich but became the defeated capital of the Second Reich, the doomed capital of the Weimar Republic, and the criminal capital of the Third Reich. By 1949 its eastern half had become a bastard capital too, of the then largely unrecognised DDR. So maybe so.

By contrast, the former West German capital, Bonn, was understated, provincial, and a little dull – perhaps well-suited to real German politics in the post-War era. Berlin is none of these and some would say that its brash dynamism has begun influencing Germany's behaviour, for example during the 2010 Euro crisis, where pragmatic self-interest appeared to many Germans to transcend the need to act for the greater good.

Karl Marx & Friedrich Engels

Where now?

The new city, arising from the ashes of its turbulent past, honours the victims of all the old Berlins in a way that no other incarnation has managed. As such it is the perfect showcase of a country that has finally come to terms with all aspects of its history and wishes to move on.

This attitude is evident throughout the city, from the Holocaust memorial in the shadow of the Brandenburg Gate to the preserved sections of the Wall. There are even plans to rebuild Berlin Castle, the residence of Prussian Kings and German Emperors for a hundred years until the DDR regime destroyed it on ideological grounds in 1950.

Daniel Libeskind, architect of the most impressive new building honouring the victims of Berlin's past – the Jewish

The Berlin Wall and Watchtower, c.1984

Museum – talks of the post-unification building spree turning the city into: "...the exemplary spiritual capital of the 21st Century, as it once was the apocalyptic symbol of 20th Century demise."

He has a point.

The New Jewish Museum

A pub crawl of all the cultures

The challenge for any intelligent beer tourist is how to pay attention to the place they are in without entirely neglecting their beverage of choice. This suggested route around the city will take roughly nine hours in total, provided all participants are well-disciplined. Breaking it into chunks may be a better option.

We suggest you start at the ultramodern steel and glass Hauptbahnhof – half shopping centre, half station – at the **Hopfingerbräu** brewpub on Level 4.

The New Hauptbahnhof

Leave the station by heading across Washington Platz, crossing the River Spree via the pedestrian bridge. Continuing along the footpath, with the new Reich Chancel lery on your right, you will come to the Platz der Republik, and the *Reichstag*.

From 1894 until 1933 the *Reichstag* housed the German parliament. It was burned down by Nazi stooges in 1933 but blamed on others, providing a convenient excuse for a purge of anti-Nazi elements.

It was from the *Reichstag* balcony, during the 1948–49 Blockade, that Mayor Ernst Reuter addressed half a million Berliners, appealing to the world for help. The result was the Berlin Airlift.

Substantial wartime damage was repaired and it was a museum until 1989, whereafter it was determined that the national parliament would return here. The glass dome, designed by UK architect Sir Norman Foster, was added in 1999.

A line of bricks just to the east of the Reichstag marks the route of the Berlin Wall. Where this hits the river is the *Weisse Kreuze* memorial, seven white crosses dedicated to the 190 people who lost their lives while trying to escape over it.

Reichstag

A pub crawl of all the cultures

There were 5,075 successful escapes in its 28-year history – 574 by border guards! Before the Wall went up in 1961, around five thousand people a week had been fleeing from the East.

Leaving the square across Scheidemannstraße, enter the *Tiergarten* park next to a café-cum-souvenir-store. There are few mature trees as most were felled for fuel during the Blockade. Following the path through the woods, turning right by a small beer garden that operates in summer, you hit Straße des 17 Juni, the date of a 1953 East Berlin uprising.

Turning right, the Soviet War Memorial to your right uses granite slabs from Hitler's Chancellery, plus two of the T-35 tanks that took part in the Battle of Berlin in 1945. This monument marks what would have been the centre of Hitler's dream capital, Germania.

Brandenburg Gate

Soviet War Memorial

Back along Straße des 17 Juni is Brandenburg Gate, the ultimate symbol of Germanic history, built in 1791. The Wall passed in front of here and it was the site of many famous Cold War speeches by Western leaders, including Ronald Reagan's famous challenge to Mikhail Gorbachev to "Tear down this wall!"

Turn right, southwards into Ebertstraße, named after Germany's first president, Friedrich Ebert (1918–25).

Heading towards Potsdamer Platz, the Holocaust Memorial on your left was completed in 2005. Officially named the "Monument to the Murdered Jews of Europe" it is made up of undulating lines of 2,711 smooth, grey-black pillars bearing no names or origins – a numbing public statement of timeless dignity, pointlessness and cold efficiency.

Walk across this memorial in a roughly diagonal direction and having reached the far corner continue south towards Gertrude Kolmar Straße. On the left is a patch of scrub waste ground. This was once the Reich Chancellery garden and the core of Third Reich Berlin. Underneath your feet was the famous bunker, the Third Reich's last stand, constructed 12 meters underground with 4-meter-thick walls, in 1944.

Just a few meters across here to your left is a small children's play area. It was here that Adolf Hitler and Eva Braun were cremated following their suicide on April 30 1945.

Walk through the gap in the apartment block into the street named 'An der Kolonade' and turn right. After a short distance turn left into Gertrude Kolmar Straße and then right into Voßstraße. At this corner,

*Potsdamer Platz –
November 2010*

on your left, was the site of Hitler's Reich Chancellery. Go down Voßstraße until you hit Ebertstraße again and turn left towards Potsdamer Platz.

Potsdamer Platz was the Piccadilly Circus of pre-war Berlin but on the front line of the Cold War. A few segments of the wall have been replaced, but the area has largely been transformed into a futuristic cityscape of offices, shops ... and two good pubs serving hearty fare to assist a return to normality: the **Lindenbräu** and **Mommseneck am Potsdamer Platz**.

Suitably refreshed, walk down Leipziger Straße, still the site of major new building works, until the junction with Wilhelmstraße, where you turn right.

*Schweinhaxe –
hearty fare*

On this corner is the building that was Goering's Aviation Ministry, the largest building in Berlin when completed in 1935 and, ironically perhaps, it was virtually untouched by wartime bombing. It later housed DDR government offices and features a socialist-realist mural on the north side. As counterpoint,

DDR Mural

there is also a reflecting pool image and memorial to the 1953 uprising, which was crushed by Soviet tanks. The building is now the Treasury.

Off Wilhelmstraße to the right is Niederkirchnerstraße, where you will find a surviving section of Berlin Wall, and a museum, the *Topographie des Terrors*, dedicated to victims of fascism and located where Himmler's SS headquarters and the Gestapo HQ once were.

A pub crawl of all the cultures

Left off Wilhelmstraße is Zimmerstraße, the site of the world's most notorious border crossing: Checkpoint Charlie. World War Three was almost triggered here in October 1961, when Soviet forces denied US troops entry into East Berlin. The ensuing tank showdown lasted three days. The rather low-key but nonetheless recommended *Haus am Checkpoint Charlie* museum recounts the many ingenious escape attempts.

A Surviving Stretch of the Berlin Wall in Niederkirchner Straße

Checkpoint Charlie

Further down Zimmerstraße, turn left into Charlottenstraße and walk five blocks to Gendarmenmarkt, the city's most elegant square, ringed by classical buildings planned by Frederick the Great. Berlin's classiest *Weihnachtsmärkt* (Christmas Market) takes place here. Although there are several smart cafés that ring the square we recommend you head to the new **Augustiner am Gendarmenmarkt**.

From the top of Gendamenmarkt, head right, eastwards into Französische Straße, then left into Hedwigskirchegasse, leading to Bebel Platz. St. Hedwig's Cathedral is Catholic, a rarity in Berlin, built by Frederick the Great for the city's Silesian population.

In the centre of Bebel Platz is a glass covered square hole perring down onto empty bookshelves, the Book Burning Monument, which commemorates the infamous events of 10th May 1933, when Nazi students and 'brown shirts', directed by Joseph Goebbels, burned 20,000 books by 'undesirable' authors.

Bebel Platz opens into majestic Unter den Linden, the main east-west axis and home to many grand buildings from the Prussian Imperial era. Just to the right across this boulevard is the *Neue Wache* or New Guard House. To the Nazis it was a hall of fame for heroes. In DDR-times it was dedicated to

Altes Museum on museum island

Gendarmenmarkt

The 'Neue Wache' in Unter den Linden

'victims of Fascism and Militarism'. Nowadays it is a memorial to all victims of war and oppression, containing a sculpture by Berlin artist Käthe Kollwitz, who lost her son in the 1914–18 War.

Heading west along Unter den Linden (towards Brandenburg Gate), past Humbolt University, turn right into Universitäts-straße by the huge bombastic statue of the man himself, Frederick the Great. This statue had been warehoused by the DDR authorities on ideological grounds, but was re-instated in the early 1980's in a less than convincing attempt to connect their regime with German history. At the elevated railway, turn right along Georgenstraße. On your left, underneath the railway, is **Deponie #3**.

Berlin Cathedral, Marienkirche & the Fernsehturm

Continuing to the end of Georgen-straße, turn right into Am Kupfergraben and follow the River Spree back to Unter den Linden. Turning left into Karl-Liebknecht-Straße and crossing the river, Berlin Cathedral and Museum Island (home to several famous museums) is to your left.

Schloßplatz to your right is currently a massive empty space but was the site of the Berlin Castle. The Communists replaced it in 1950 with the monstrous, asbestos-riddled, steel and glass Palace of the Republic, dubbed 'Erich's Lamp Store' by locals after DDR leader Erich Honecker and the thousands of lamps in its foyer.

Across Schloßplatz is the former DDR State Council building that incorporates a portal salvaged from the Schloss. It was from this balcony that Karl Liebnecht announced the birth of the (ill-fated and short-lived) German Socialist Republic in the dying days of World War 1. From this same balcony, in August 1914, Kaiser Wilhelm assured the assembled crowd that the soldiers about to leave for the front would be "home by Christmas."

After crossing a second branch of the river, pass beneath Karl-Liebknecht-

Straße into Marx-Engels Forum – a field of ruins in 1945 in which only the shell of the now restored Marienkirche survived.

Time for another beer. Five excellent pubs await in the restored Nikolaiviertel to the south of the Forum and we suggest the **Alt-Berliner Weissbierstube**.

On leaving, head right, eastwards towards Alexanderplatz, past the *Rotes Rathaus* (Red City Hall) named for its brickwork rather than its political masters. Aim for the unmissable 368m-tall Fernsehturm tower – the second tallest man-made structure in Europe, completed in 1969. If there is no queue, take a detour up to the revolving viewing platform.

Down at ground level are two brewpubs. Closer is the cavernous **Brauhaus Mitte**, while **Marcus Brau** is around the corner in Münzstraße.

Heading up Dirksenstraße and following the railway to Hackescher Markt you will come to the Hackeschen Höfe, a series of beautifully preserved, intricately tiled courtyards – now mostly graphic design studios and chic restaurants. On exiting these, turn right along Oranienburger Straße and right again into Große Hamburger Straße.

(above) Fernsehturm and Marienkirche

The Restored Nikolaiviertel

Hackeschen Höfe

On the right is an old Jewish Cemetery, used as a transit camp by the Nazis for those being transported to Auschwitz. Nearby is a rare sight in central Berlin – an unrestored building, still bullet-scarred from 1945.

A Battle-Scarred Building in Große Hamburger Straße

All the pubs on our tour so far serve good food but if you can save your appetite for here, try to do so, as a few metres further up is the fabulous **Sophie'n Eck**.

Retracing your steps, take a right into Krausnickstraße then right again at Oranienburger Straße. On the right is the New Synagogue, which avoided destruction during the Kristallnacht pogrom of November 9 1938 thanks to Wilhelm Krutzfeld, a police officer who bravely drew his pistol to ward off the arsonists.

A bit further along, on the left it is impossible to miss 'Tachles', an alternative art squat under threat of demolition. An exciting addition to Berlin's cultural milieu or a malodorous eyesore? Make up your own mind.

Almost opposite in Linienstraße, just before Oranienburger Tor, is the excellent **Gambrinus**, which is open until late, so you could be forgiven for ending here.

However, for the final leg, should you have any legs left, head down Friedrichstraße and cross the river to Friedrichstraße station, the site of the main border crossing for West Berliners visiting relatives in the East after the Wall went up. Here the Stasi border guards inspected passports and demanded a compulsory exchange of DM25 into worthless *Ostmarks*. From the S-Bahn platform you can see the *Tränenpalast* (or Palace of Tears), a flimsy-looking pre-fabricated building outside of which so many tearful partings occured, as relatives from the East could go no further.

Contemplate in the **Berliner Republik** on Schiffbauerdamm, then go home.

Tachles – alternative art squat in Oranienburg Straße

Getting there

Berlin-Brandenburg International (BBI) airport will open in 2012, after which Tegel and Schönefeld Airports will shut. A fast shuttle train will leave BBI every 15 minutes, reaching the Hauptbahnhof in 17 minutes, stopping only at Südkreutz and Potsdamer Platz.

Travel from the two existing airports is less accommodating. There is no rail connection at Tegel, though airport buses go to Alexanderplatz and the U-Bahnhof (U8 & U9) at Osloerstrasse.

From Schönefeld there are S-Bahn lines (S9 & S45) but these do not go near the centre. From the S9 heading east and north, change at Ostkreutz; while the S45 terminates at Bundesplatz, connecting with several U-Bahn lines on the way. Infrequent regional trains do go through Alexanderplatz and Hauptbahnhof on their way from Schönefeld to Charlottenburg or Spandau.

A taxi from Tegel to the centre is around €25; from Schönefeld more like €40 – worth it for small parties with luggage.

Being there

Travelling around Berlin is cheap and simple.

The same tickets cover the U-Bahn 🄤 (underground railway), S-Bahn 🅢 (overground railway), bus 🚌 and tram 🄗 networks. These are extensive and most services run every 5 to 10 minutes, though less frequently at night and at weekends.

Additionally a comprehensive network of night buses and most U-Bahn lines run half-hourly services throughout the wee small hours.

Zones A & B cover all 80 entres in this guide, but not Schönefeld airport. In 2011, day tickets valid on all forms of public transport cost just €6,30 and for 5 days €28,90; on the other hand a single fare (valid for two hours) cost €2,30 and a four-journey card €8,20. At weekends, two can travel for the price of one. For a real bargain, a small group (up to 4) day ticket is only €15. All tickets must be validated at the time of first usage in the yellow machines at all platforms or stops.

Tickets can be bought from machines at stations and in all trams. These can seem intimidating at first and tend to behave better with coins than notes. Tickets are also available from manned kiosks at larger stations and from some newsagent kiosks. There are no barriers – just an army of plain-clothes inspectors who treat freeriders with little compassion. While you may go a week without being asked to produce a valid ticket, we have been checked twice in one day.

Where to stay?

Craft beer fans would love the cool, idiosyncratic charm of the defiantly 'non-chain' Circus Hotel in Rosenthaler Platz (0049 30 2000 3939; info@ circus-berlin.de) For those on a tighter budget, try their Hostel (same contact details) just opposite.

In the late 19th Century there were 200 breweries in Berlin, many of which traded throughout Germany. The economic woes during and after the two 20th Century wars coupled with the artificial isolation of West Berlin after 1945 put paid to most of that and by by 1989 there were just two left in the west – Schultheiss in Kreutzberg and Kindl in Neukölln – and five in the East.

The eastern five were grouped together under state control as a *Combinat* and sold after reunification as a job lot to Bräu und Brunnen, a large West German holding company later absorbed into the Dr Oetker group, now rebranded Radeberger Gruppe, which currently holds 15% of the German beer market.

At one point six of the seven Berlin breweries that were there when the wall came down were owned by the same group, which decided to close five of them, with all production concentrated at a site renamed the Berliner Kindl Schultheiss Brewery (BKS).

BKS churns out 1.6 million hectolitres of beer a year, in 28 different varieties. All use the same Hallertau hop pellets and soft well water, which is hardened before use. However, they remain all-malt and each beer is fermented with its own carefully chosen yeast strain.

Three beer brands make up 80% of production – the ubiquitous but drinkable, dry and bitter Berliner Pils, the slightly sweeter Berliner Kindl Pils and the yet

The Berliner-Kindl-Schultheiss (BKS) Brewery

19

softer and sweeter Schultheiss Pils. The other 25 include everything under the Kindl brand, the sole remaining Berliner Weisse, Englehardt Pils, Potsdamer Rex Pils, and the remorselessly sweet Märkisches Landmann Schwarzbier.

The remaining non-BKS brewery was the Berliner Burgerbräu Brewery (BBB) in the eastern suburb of Köpenick. But it now has also sadly been gobbled up by the Radeburger Gruppe with its interesting beers, such as Premium Pils, Bernauer Schwarzbier, Rotkehlchen, Weissbier, and a couple of seasonal Bocks moving to BKS. Still, they have not lost their sparkle and remain a cut above most other output from BKS.

Its future is unclear. BBB occupies prime real estate on the shores of the Müggelsee, so future redevelopment into executive apartments seems inevitable. However there is also a plan to restart brewing at BBB in 2012, on a micro level.

The BKS plant is a craft beer lover's nightmare but worth visiting in a perverse way. The sheer scale is awe-inspiring and the bottling hall is a wonder of engineering. Tours in German (Mo–Th only) are (2011) €4,00 per head or €5,00 with one beer; or €12,00 with a meal and unlimited beer. Tours in English can be arranged (contact T +49 30 9609 579, or E c.tieze@radeberger-gruppe.de).

Fortunately, Berlin's brewing history does not end here, and there has been an explosion of new brewpubs. They now officially number 17 (although only 14 actually appear to brew on the premises). Most serve excellent food, too.

Another positive event has been a resumption of brewing at the old Kindl brewery by the new Rollberg micro-brewery, which makes three unfiltered, highly drinkable brews. Try them all at

Berliner Bürgerbräu Brewery in Köpenick – Closed in 2009

the brewery tap (Werbellin Straße 50 – shut Su–Th; Fr from 17.00; Sa from 15.00), 300 metres from U7 Rathaus Neukölln. Free tours are available on Saturdays at 16.00.

Virtually all German breweries still follow the old Bavarian *Reinheitsgebot* (or Beer Purity Law), which was ruled anticompetitive by the EU in 1987 and formally withdrawn from the state statute book.

This ancient edict, introduced in 1512, restricted the ingredients that may be

The old Kindl Brewery in Neukölln – now home to the Rollberg microbrewery.

*Rollberg Brewery –
inside the old Berliner
Kindl Brewery*

used in making beer to malted barley, hops, water and yeast. A later amendment allowed wheat too but only in certain circumstances. Approved breweries were allowed to continue making wheat beers for the elite, but it was dictated that "in their best interests" the peasant class should preserve their own wheat for bread.

It was as part of a general clean up of German brewing, which suffered from poor quality at the time. It also had the effect of supporting brewing monopolies held by feudal lords and princes in that by outlawing the use of herbs, spices and other grains it forced many independent brewers out of business.

One major effect of this law was to prevent German beer culture developing along the lines of Belgium and elsewhere, where a spectacular range of regional variations survive.

The idea that the *Reinheitsgebot* was an entirely good thing guaranteeing best quality entered the German psyche in much the same way that in recent years we British have become absolutist in

believing that all good beer must be refer-mented in its cask or bottle by live yeast.

The inadvertent effect has been that while German beers are usually of high quality, they can become boringly repetitive. Even today, many brewers offer nothing beyond a Helles (light) and a Dunkles (dark).

Despite the fact that a quarter of a century has passed since the *Reinheitsgebot* was withdrawn, it is only recently that brewers have felt confident to experiment with new styles and ingredients. Thankfully, this includes most of the brewpubs in Berlin, all of which are featured below.

A boarded-up pub in Charlottenburg.

Altbier or Alt

A style synonymous with Düsseldorf, although 'Old Beer' is now brewed elsewhere, throughout Germany. A style of top-fermented and reddish brown beer, similar to many pre-War British bitters in recipe and fermentation, but cold-conditioned as a lager to smoothe out its craggier edges. The alcohol content is standardly a precise 4.8%. A good Alt will have roasted malt and dry fruit flavours, with a bitter hop finish.

Berliner Weisse

Low-alcohol, sourish wheat beer that can likely trace its ancestry back over a thousand years to the days of Charlemagne, when a culture of different types of wheat beer was spread acoss much of Central Europe.

Red (or rot) Berliner Weisse

In modern times the sole example has been brewed under the Kindl label, currently by BKS, and nowhere else.

However, on holiday in New Orleans just days before this guide went to the printers, your author tasted another Berliner Weisse called "Professor Fritz Briem's 1809 Berliner Weisse", which was superior to Kindl Weisse (drier, tarter and vinous, like a good sparkling hock). This beer is brewed by the eponymous professor at the Doemans Institute, part of the famous brewing university at Freising, Bavaria. Why we have never seen it in Berlin (even at Weihenstephaner) remains a mystery.

Most Berliners drink Berliner Weisse mixed with raspberry (*rot*) or woodruff (*grün*) syrup to mask the very tartness that makes it refreshing. We advise it is drunk *ohne Schuß* – literally 'without excess baggage'.

Bockbier or Bock

A stronger style, usually 7% or above, which originated in the northern town of Einbeck in the Middle Ages, but has spread across Europe and now America in various forms. Can be anywhere between dark golden to jet-black. Often brewed as a seasonal special, for example Maibock for spring. The autumnal variety became popular as ways of seeing off leftover malt from the previous year when the new harvest was in. Weizenbock contains both wheat and malted barley. Doppelbock is ultrastrong.

Dunkles, Dunkelbier or Schwarzbier

'Dark' or 'black' beers can be anywhere from pale brown to black. The same strength as Pilsener and Helles (5%), some are actually Helles with colouring. A good Dunkel should have roasted malt and caramel flavours with a hint of chocolate or coffee. Some have a dry, bitter finish like a stout, whilst others finish with more fruitiness.

Helles, Hellesbier or Hell

This is the name applied to any pale beer, though most frequently a blond lager. Alcohol is always around 5% and the taste should be light, with some malt and variable hop presence, ranging from soft to harsh and crispy to soapy. Some are a little more robust, especially those from microbreweries or brewpubs that often serve them unfiltered (*natürtrub*).

Kellerbier

A low-carbonation, unfiltered amber beer, less fizzy than a Pilsner due to the gas being allowed to leak slightly from the barrel in the cellar. Originally a speciality from around Bamberg, in Franconia, it is now made in many more places. It should be dry and hoppy and is often served in a stone jug (*Krug*) to hide the natural haziness.

Kölsch

No beer has yet earned the Protected Designation of Origin (PDO) that winemakers display as 'Appelation Contrôlée', but this beer style from Köln (Cologne) has managed the Protected Geographical Indication (PGI), which at least means that one of the stages of production, processing or preparation must be in or around that area. Pale gold and around 4.8%, it should be light, crisp and fruity, with some having more malt in the balance. It may look like a lager but is fermented as an ale. It should be served in a small (preferably 20cl), narrow, straight glass alled a *Stange*, with a dense, long-lasting *Schaum* (or head).

Sion Kölsch

Märzen

The equivalent of Belgian 'saison', these slightly stronger than average lagers were traditionally brewed in March for consumption in the summer, before the days of refridgeration, when beer fermentation on hot days was fraught with the danger of spoiling. Nowadays it tends just to mean a slightly stronger, often copper-coloured brew, which has started to appear as an annual special in many brewpubs in, er, March each year.

German beer styles

Pilsner or Pils

The all-powerful beer style that originated in Bohemia (now the Czech Republic) and now accounts for two-thirds of all the beer drunk in Germany. Pilsners are golden, ranging from pale straw to honey amber and hover around the 5% mark.

North German pilsners are dry and hoppy, with the very best verging on herbal in flavour. South German pilsners are maltier, sweeter and sometimes stronger. Cool-fermented over at least ten days and then cold-conditioned for six to twelve weeks, any such lager made with 100% malt and good quality hopping will be good and some are spectacular. Most of the world's industrial lagers and a few better known German brands disobey these rules in order to cut corners and end pretty insipid, fully earning the poor reputation they enjoy among knowledgeable beer drinkers.

Krombacher Pils

Rauchbier

Strongly associated with and mostly still brewed in the Franconian beer paradise of Bamberg, these carefully made lagers are brewed using a proportion of malt that is smoked over a beechwood furnace, giving the beer a distinctive 'smoked

meat' character. This addition can be made to any style of beer and Bamberg brewers between them produce Helles and Dunles lagers, Kellerbier, Märzen and Weisse beers in this style. If you like smoky bacon crisps, you will love these.

Weizenbier, Weizen, Weissbier or Weisse

A proper Bavarian 'white beer' brewed from roughly one-third unmalted wheat, two-thirds malted barley and then top-fermented. The wheat lends the beer a dough-like sweetness and in unfiltered form leaves a fine floury haze. These Bavarian brews are generally stronger than their Berlin counterpart and can be highly carbonated. Depending on which strain(s) of yeast are used to ferment them they can take on a lemony character and/or a strong banana flavour. In their unfiltered state they are usually known as Hefeweizen or Hefeweisse, filtered versions being known as Kristal. Darker versions go by the confusing desription of Dunkel Weiss, or similar, meaning 'Brown White' or 'Dark White'. It was this style of beer that led the beer-drinking counter-culture in Germany, while the British were discovering 'real ale' and the rest of the world 'craft beer'. Stronger Bock versions appear too. In Bavaria it is challenging Pilsner as the favourite style of beer.

Zwickelbier

Applying this term to any German beer embues it with a suggestion of traditional authenticity, though in truth it is a term of fairly recent origin and can mean anything from a short-run seasonal beer perhaps from a shortened fermentation period, as with British cask bitter, or simply an unfiltered, young or 'green' beer. They tend to be fresh, spritzy and tart.

This annual monster-fest takes place on the second weekend of August each year along Karl Marx Allee (formerly Stalin Allee) to the east of the city centre, stretching for a full mile between Frankfurter Tor and Stausberger Platz, thus earning its German title of *Der Goldene Meile*.

Around 250 breweries pay for space and set up their own bars, arranged geographically and offering almost 2,000 different beers. There are also 18 live music stages dotted along the route assisting, if assistance were needed, a party atmosphere that can get pretty lively. For the beer lover the problem is that in among the selection are hundreds of seriously dull beers, many from round the world.

BBF in Full Swing

Is the UK really best represented by John Smith's Smooth Flow – we think not.

Sadly, at €3,500 per stand, smaller and more innovative microbrewers simply cannot afford to attend. Perhaps if they banded together ...?

Worth the craic but be sure to take a reference book with you, such as Steve Thomas's *Good Beer Guide Germany* (also from **www.booksaboutbeer.com**), in order to choose wisely.

Beer strength – a disclaimer

72 of the 80 beers we list are on draught and there is no German law obliging pubs to state alcohol content on the tap. The alcohol percentages we quote are those that we understand to be prevailing at the time we went to press. As a basic rule, a typical German beer will contain around 5% alcohol by volume, with Berliner Weisse coming in at 3.5% and Bocks and Doppelbocks hitting 7% and upwards.

❶ Alkopole Bierbar 🍴 🥨
Bahnhof Alexanderplatz, 10178 Berlin-Mitte
T 030 2472 9970
www.alkopole.de
🍴 Snacks only
Ⓤ U2, U5 & U8 (Alexanderplatz)
Ⓢ S3, S5, S7, S75 (Alexanderplatz)
🕐 Mo–Sa 09.00–01.00; Su 10.00–22.00

This small, cosy, basic boozers' den is inside busy Alexanderplatz station (the "Alex" in Berlin slang). There are entrances by the escalators down from the S-Bahn platforms (opposite a tobacconist) and from the street by the M2 tram stop.

The Alkopole is a great place to observe Berlin life. The pub seats no more than forty, but this larva becomes a butterfly in summer, spilling out into a comfortable pavement beer garden. Inside, the turnover of patrons is quite rapid as drinkers rush off to catch trains. There is a Wurlitzer Jukebox in one corner and a faux tree in another, backed by a colourful beer garden mural – a valiant attempt to impart a little country flavour. The snack menu has a dozen different sausages and boulettes (Berlin meatballs), all served with 'mixed pickle'.

The pub boasts a reasonable beer selection, albeit dominated by the Radeberger Group, including Radeberger Pils, Kapuziner Weissbier Hell, Berliner Kindl Jubiläums Pilsner, and the black, dry, roastiness of **Berliner Kindl Bock Dunkel** (7%), available in winter when it replaces the Jubiläums Pilsner.

There are also about 15 bottled beers on offer, including Newcastle Brown! In summer, try Mönchshof Kellerbier from a flip-top bottle, a reddish-brown, unfiltered, bottle-fermented beer that is mild and refreshing. Other bottle options include Diebels Alt and Erdinger Pikantus Weizenbock. The schnapps and spirits list runs to about 50, making this a good bar for chasers.

Alois S

② Alois S ✖ 🏵
Senefelder Straße 18, 10437 Berlin-Prenzlauerberg
T 030 4471 9680
www.AloisS.de
🍴 Full menu, Spanish tapas a speciality
Ⓢ S8, S9, S41 & S42 (Prenzlauer Allee)
Ⓗ M2 (Fröbel Straße)
🕐 Winter: Mo–Sa 18.00–02.00, Su 10.00–02.00
   Summer: Mo–Fr 15.00–02.00, Sa 13.00–02.00, Su 10.00–02.00

Prenzlauerberg is a rapidly gentrifying district of Berlin and home to several establishments such as this – cool, bare, understated chic with a Spanish menu. The mosaic floor and Art Deco 'cathode-ray tube' wall lighting complete the picture. The pub is on the corner of Stargarder Straße, very close to the Thüringer Stuben (below), and has a large children's play area out in front.

The beer selection is excellent and features Wernesgruner Pils, Rothaus Tannenzäpfle Pils, Augustiner Helles, and our choice, **Augustiner Edelstoff** (5.6%) on draught. This is one of the author's all-time favourite German beers, with a brewery grain aroma and a huge malty mouth-feel, smooth with complex fruit flavours (lychee and pear) emerging. A perfect balance leaves a lingering aftertaste of all the above, without any sharp bitterness notes to intrude.

The bottled beer selection also has a Bavarian slant, featuring Augustiner Hefeweisse, Franziskaner Hefeweisse, Kloster Andechs Dunkel Hefeweisse, Rothaus Tannenzäpfle Hefeweisse, Augustiner Dunkel, Beck's, and a beer of the week – usually a Bavarian Kloster (abbey) beer. For a Spanish beer to go with the tapas, try **Estrella Galicia**. As you might expect, the wine and cocktail lists are also impressive.

Alte Kolkshenke

3 **Alte Kolkshenke** 🍺 ⬅
Kolk 3, 13597 Berlin-Spandau
T 030 333 3762
🍺 None
U U7 (Altstadt Spandau)
S S75 (Spandau)
⊗ Wednesday
🕐 Others 17.00–24.00 (closing time may vary)

We're not sure which century formed this pub, but it's certainly not this one or the last. The Alte Kolkshenke is a tiny, time-warp boozer in the Spandau Alt Stadt, and how the building in which it resides is still standing is a mystery. Approaching it, you could be forgiven for thinking it must have closed down years ago. Thankfully it has not, living to be a magnificent survivor from another age.

From the U-Bahnhof take Breite Straße, turn around and head north for a few metres until you reach the main road, Am Juliusturm. Cross this and head down the small flight of steps opposite. The street called Kolk is on your left after a few metres, and the pub is 50 metres down on your left.

The café is dark with wood panels, a low bar with a mirrored rear wall, loads of ancient bric-a-brac, and pictures and maps of old Spandau, which was already a sizeable town back when Berlin was a mere pup of a village.

The old lady who runs this place could well also be from the century in which it was founded, so don't expect rapid service. There is just the one beer on draft, **Berliner Kindl Pils** (4.6%), a very light, straw-gold lager from BKS, a drinkable pilsner with a sweetish, vanilla malt character, if perhaps lacking a little bitterness in the finish.

Ambrosius Bier Club

④ Ambrosius Bier Club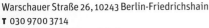
Warschauer Straße 26, 10243 Berlin-Friedrichshain
T 030 9700 3714
www.ambrosius-bier-club.de
None
U U1 (Warschauer Straße)
S S3, S5, S7 & S75 (Warschauer Straße)
⊗ Sunday
Mo–Th 16.00-01.00; Fr–Sa 16.00–03.00

This really is a beer club, though anyone can join. You get a club card and the more you drink, the cheaper it becomes. (That's not just alcohol befuddling your brain). The €110,00 Gold Card entitles you to 144 0.3l bevvies, which at €0,76 a pop means one-third of the normal price. Of course it may take you a while to drink them all ....

The Ambrosius is a large, lively, loud and basic drinking den that doubles as the supporters club for the Berliner Eisbaren (Polar Bears) ice hockey team, who play in the nearby O2 arena. The pub features an odd mix of tiles, ceramic display boxes, an antique motorised bicycle and old beer adverts. It is also a popular live music venue, and a big screen makes this a good place to watch sport, especially if you like ice hockey.

The beer attractions include three specially commissioned from the Meininger Privatbrauerei in Thüringen. These are Ambrosius Pils, Ambrosius Dunkel, and **Ambrosius Export** (5.2%), which is sweetish, low on hops and has a full mouth feel, with some bitterness in the finish. Seasonal beers are also offered – a Maibock in spring, a dark Bock in December, and a 3.5% **Landbier** (like a UK dark mild) in the summer. Other draught beers are Berliner Pils, Berliner Kindl Jubiläums Pils and Radeberger Pils, but the seven bottled options are of limited appeal.

Alt-Berliner Weissbierstube

5 **Alt-Berliner Weissbierstube** 🍴 ✖ ❄
Rathaus Straße 21, 10178 Berlin-Mitte
T 030 242 4454
🍽 Full menu with Berlin specialities
Ⓤ U2 (Klosterstraße)
Ⓢ S3, S5, S7 & S75 (Alexanderplatz)
Ⓗ M4, M5 & M6 (Marienkirche)
🕐 Daily 11.00–24.00

Despite its city centre location, the 'Old Berlin White Beer Pub', an excellent and authentic recreation of an old Berlin drinking den, is not easily reached by public transport, though an extension of the U5 line should soon rectify this.

A small outside drinking area overlooks Marx-Engels Forum; a charming lobby has a wicker chair and an etched glass door; and the pub itself is cosy, plush, smart and decorated with numerous artefacts including pictures and maps. For 1890s-style pornography, check out the saucy prints in the far room. Beyond the bar in both directions are restaurant areas, some of them private, while the raised leather bench seat to one side of the bar is one of the best perches for drinking beer (or schnapps) in all Berlin.

Ignore its other beers, since as its name suggests, this is *the* place to try **Berliner Kindl Weisse** (3%). Now only available in bottles from BKS, this can feel slightly insipid initially on its own, a bit like a diluted, sweet Belgian lambic. Thus it is usually served *rot* (red: with raspberry syrup), or *grün* (green: with minty woodruff flavouring). If you must add one of these, we suggest the latter, though here at the Stube they also serve Berliner Weisse in eight different styles, including with Blue Curacao, or with Champagne and lemon! Order Kirschwasser schnapps as a chaser – as good here as anywhere.

6 Augustiner am Gendarmenmarkt
Charlotten Straße 55, 10117 Berlin-Mitte
T 030 2045 4020
www.augustiner-braeu-berlin.de
Full menu with a Bavarian slant
U2 & U6 (Stadtmitte)
Daily 10.00–02.00

It was a while coming, but it has finally arrived: a 'genuine' Bavarian beer hall in the centre of Berlin. Situated on the corner of Jäger Straße, this enjoys a prime location right in the heart of the German capital, but the musty ambiance, large windows, décor and furniture are pure Munich. There may even be a resident 'oompah' band as well, although thus far we have successfully avoided this.

The pavement seating does not afford the best view of the Gendarmenmarkt because the pub is tucked behind the Konzerthaus Theatre, but you can see the impressive Französisches Dom, one of Schinkel's finest buildings.

Augustiner is among the best of the large Munich breweries, though this pub sadly does not sell the full range. Draught beers are Augustiner Helles, Augustiner Edelstoff – served from a *Holzfass* (wooden barrel) daily from 18.00 – and Augustiner Dunkel, their least appealing creation, copper-red with a malty,

dry but sharp and sour taste, often served far too cold. Oktoberfestbier is only offered in season; late September and, naturally, October.

Alas, the Starkbierzeit offering, Maximator, is not available at any time. This is brewed for the Munich Starkbierzeit, an annual spring festival that means, literally, a 'time for strong beer'.

We recommend instead that you go for bottled **Augustiner Pils** (5.6%), a straw-coloured, dry and full-bodied pilsner with hints of citrus.

31

7 Bechereck
Okker Straße 35, 12049 Berlin-Neukölln
T 0176 6082 8836
Breakfast and limited snacks
U U8 (Leinestraße)
24 hours a day

The open-all-hours Bechereck is a classic Berlin corner local in an area where more of these pubs seem to survive than in other districts. It sits on the corner of Schillerpromenade, close to the eastern fringes of what used to be Tempelhof Airport.

On the outside walls, overlooking some pavement seating, are some fabulous Breugel-esque murals of locals drinking, dancing and making merry. Inside, the main bar is small, cosy and cramped. Note the pewter measuring jug collection and the vegetation-themed stained glass windows. A larger bar at the back contains a billiard table.

The owner is a Russian lady, Marina Kremlerskaja from St Petersburg, who is also an artist. She is responsible for the 3-D boxed ceramic artefacts dotted all over the place, which have a certain innocent charm.

Bechereck serves two draught beers, a dark, sweet Czech lager, and **Ambrosius Pils** (5%), a pale yellow, soft, spicy and biscuity pilsner, with a real hoppy bitter tang in the finish, from the Meininger Brewery in Thüringen. Five bottled options complete the picture: Schultheiss Pils, Berliner Kindl Pils, Beck's, the refreshing Erdinger Hefeweisse, and Baltika, a lager from the landlady's home town.

Berliner Republik

8 Berliner Republik
Schiffbauerdamm 8, 10117 Berlin-Mitte
T 030 3087 2293
www.die-berliner-republik.de
Full menu with a Berlin slant
U6 (Friedrichstraße)
S3, S5, S7 & S75 (Friedrichstraße)
Daily 11.00–04.00 (from 10.00 in summer)

Next door to the Ständige Vertretung, which laments German reunification and the establishment of Berlin as the capital, this large, lively place celebrates the opposite and calls itself, deliberately no doubt, the "capital city pub", rubbing it in with a biblical mural depicting Christ being reunited with God after the resurrection, and the words Willi Brand spoke the day after the Wall came down, "Now let us join together what belongs together."

Perhaps uniquely, the prices of the twenty draught beers here change constantly like a stock exchange – the *Bier Börse*

– TV screens displaying the latest. If you buy a round of one particular beer, watch its price shoot up. Prices fluctuate between maximum and minimum levels, the screens turning red when they fall and green when they rise. Grey means no recent changes. The exchange opens at 19.00 each evening, but the staff will turn it on early if you ask nicely. A well-timed purchase can save quite a bit and every so often the market 'crashes', all prices falling to their minimum, sparking frenzied 'panic' buying.

If you can take your eyes off the trading screens, check out the recent but historical pictures and memorabilia decorating the walls. Smokers should try the yellow telephone kiosks (*raucher kabinen*), decorated with pictures of former Chancellors puffing away.

The house beer, Schiffbauer Pils is pretty bland. Go instead for **Bayreuther Zwickl Kellerbier** (5.3%), a fresh, unfiltered and yeasty 'young' beer; dry, tart and citric, not dissimilar to a young Belgian lambic. It is served in a stone jug, or *Krug*.

⑨ **Bier Spezialitäten-Laden** 🏧
Karl-Marx Allee 56, 10243 Berlin-Friedrichshain
T 030 249 2146
🍴 None
Ⓤ U5 (Strausberger Platz)
⊗ Sunday
🕐 Mo–Fr 10.00–19.30; Sa 10.00–14.30

The 'Beer Speciality Shop' is the best beer shop in the city, a cornucopia of delights with over 500 bottled varieties – of which over 300 are German.

There are nooks and crannies everywhere, and a back room crammed floor-to-ceiling with bottles. The place is reminiscent of some the better beer shops found in Belgium, but with a more cosmopolitan and international flavour.

From all of these (and we admit to not having tried them all!) the choice is **Kyritzer Mord und Totschlag** (7.2%), a hard-to-find beer that translates literally as "murder and manslaughter", but which can also mean 'blood and thunder' in colloquial German.

It is a morbid name for a beer that is anything but that way inclined. This strong bock-style beer, jet black, smooth and dry, is robust like a stout but with prune and raisin dried fruit flavours in the finish, like a good porter. Definitely one for the suitcase on the journey home.

Also in the vicinity, and on the U5 metro line, is the Brewery Fan Shop (Pettenkoferstraße 48, 100m north of U-Bahnhof Frankfurter Allee) on the way to the excellent new Schalander brewpub (below). It sells all kinds of Berlin beer memorabilia and merchandise, though beware that the XL size is smaller than its counterpart in the UK, and XXL garments are rare – odd given the size of many German beer drinkers.

Bornholmer Hütte
Bornholmer Straße 89, 10439 Berlin-Prenzlauerberg
T 030 445 5269
Diverse snacks
U2 (Schönhauser Allee)
S8, S9, S41 & S42 (Schönhauser Allee)
M1 & M13 (Bornholmer Straße & Schönhauser Allee)
Daily 10.00–04.00

Anyone pining nostalgically for the loss of all the old East End London boozers should head straight here. This is a down-to-earth, East Berlin locals' *kneipe*, founded in 1911. It is likely still frequented by former border guards from the nearby Bornholmer Straße crossing point, which was the first to be breached when the Wall came down.

Named the 'Bornholm Hut' in 1954, the pub remained in private hands throughout the communist era. The décor is pure nicotine, the furnishings bare, with an impressive bar, frayed red lino flooring and a sailing ship lampshade. Pool, darts and a bowling alley in the basement might tempt the more active.

Draught beers include Schultheiss Pils and Berliner Pils, along with a sweetish dark Czech offering called Jarosover. A good bottled range includes Gaffel Kölsch, Becks Gold, Neuzeller Schwartzer Abt

(a jet-black, sweet, thin abbey-style beer tasting of candy sugar and little else), Wernesgrüner Pils, Radeberger Pils, Flensburger Pils, the best widely available dark beer Köstrizer Schwarzbier and Berliner Weisse.

Our choice is the consistently excellent **Erdinger Weißbier Dunkel** (5.6%) from Erding, just outside Munich. This dry, wheaty and roasty creation with banana and vanilla flavours may not be the locals' choice, but is a perfect accompaniment for the limited and simple food offerings, including Berliner boulette, potato salad, chilli, rollmop herring, Bockwurst and Knackerwurst.

11 **Brauhaus Bohnsdorf** ✕ ♟ ❀ ☕
Buntzel Straße 89, 12526 Berlin-Treptow
T 030 676 7913
www.brauhaus-bohnsdorf.de
Ⓟ Local specialities
Ⓢ S9 & S45 (Mo–Fr only) (Alt-Glienicke – 1km away)
Ⓑ 163 from the S-Bahnhof at Schönefeld airport
⊗ Tuesday
🕐 We–Mo 11.30–23.00

Of all the pubs in the guide, this is the furthest from the city centre by some distance. Although out in *die Bohndocke* and not easy to get to the journey is worthwhile, both for the interesting house-brewed beers and the simple scrubbed-pine country charm of the décor.

From Alt-Glienicke S-Bahn walk up the steps from the platform and turn right onto a bridge over the main road. Then turn right again and follow the footpath round, bearing left, until it merges with a road from the right. Follow this for 600 metres until you reach Buntzel Straße on your left. The pub is 200 metres down on your right.

Although this is a brewpub, its brewing kit is off-limits, kept behind closed doors in the cellar. As its landlady explains, "This is not a show brewery". Downstairs, a small cellar bar with a TV, for smokers, opens much later than the main bar.

The pub also offers Wernesgruner Pils and Berliner Pils on draught plus the two house beers. Bohnsdorf Helles is a dark gold lager, full and robust with strong honey flavours, and some tartness in the finish. Our preference is **Bohnsdorf Dunkel** (5.8%), a deep brown beer with a creamy, rich mouth-feel and caramel and roast flavours, finishing bittersweet without the tart notes of the Helles.

⑫ **Brauhaus Mitte**
Karl Liebknecht-Straße 13, 10178 Berlin-Mitte
T 030 3087 8989
www.brauhaus-mitte.de
🍴 Bavarian specialities
Ⓤ U2, U5 & U8 (Alexanderplatz)
Ⓢ S3, S5, S7 & S75 (Alexanderplatz)
🕐 Daily 11.00–24.00

This Bavarian-themed brewpub is now part of the expanding Lemke empire, though it has yet to be renamed as such. Brauhaus Mitte is huge, sprawling and modern, on the first floor of a shopping centre but strangely atmospheric nonetheless. Its outside terrace is a wonderful spot to watch the world go by.

Trains thunder continuously, sometimes as many as five in a minute, over the viaduct into and out of Alexanderplatz station, making this a dream destination for beer-loving train spotters. (Note: S-Bahn trains are square and chubby with distinctive red and mustard colours; regional DB trains are predominately red and often double-decker; while the high-speed ICE trains are sleek and creamy white with a red stripe. And that's as far as our train-spotting skills go.)

If trains are not your thing, try the Motorcycle Museum underneath the railway arches opposite.

Four draught beers are usually available. The Pilsner is (probably) filtered, pale and creamy; the Dunkel is thin and sweet with roast flavours; and the seasonal offering can be a Zwickelbier. Best of all is **Brauhaus Mitte Hefeweisse Hell** (5%), a yeasty, chewy, toffee-flavoured beer with banana and bitter cranberry in the finish. A hugely interesting beer in contrast to the other two mainstays.

⑬ Brauhaus in Rixdorf ✪ ❀
Glasower Straße 27, 12051 Berlin-Neukolln
T 030 626 8880
www.Brauhaus-Rixdorf.de
🍽 Full menu including local specialities
Ⓤ U7 (Grenzallee) or U8 (Hermannstraße)
Ⓢ S41, S42, S45 (Mo–Fr only), S47 (Hermannstraße)
⊗ Monday
🕐 Tu–Sa 12.00–01.00; Su 10.00–23.00

This oasis in a run-down part of town is a little difficult
to find since it occupies a space between Glasower
Straße and Delbruch Straße. This was once a well-
established brewpub (1988) in an attractive suburban
villa dating from 1885 but no longer brews any beer.

The Brauhaus spreads over several
large rooms and has an old country-
house feel. Visit on a fine day in
summer and you can choose a shady
spot under the vine trellises in the
rambling, overgrown beer garden.

It is worth combining your visit with some of the other excellent pubs in the area and a trip
to nearby Tempelhof (U6 – Platz der Luftbrücke), the old airport. Its stunning Art Deco terminal
building was originally built by the Nazis and only closed to passenger traffic in 2008.

A prominent memorial to the British and American airmen who died during
the Berlin Airlift sits on the road junction by the U-Bahnhof.

Brewing may have stopped, but the names of the two beers
remain. Rixdorfer Dunkel tastes of chocolate but is as thin and
watery as cream soda. **Rixdorfer Hell** (5.2%) on the other hand
is a pale golden lager with a sharp, bitter taste that lingers in
the finish. Our spies tell us that they are brewed somewhere
in Brandenburg but we do not know where. On our last visit,
both were served in Hacker-Pschorr glasses from Munich,
which may mean nothing.

⑭ Brauhaus in Spandau
Neuendorfer Straße 1, 13585 Berlin-Spandau
T 030 353 9070
www.brauhaus-spandau.de
Full menu
U7 (Altstadt Spandau)
S75 (Spandau)
Fifteen, including 130 and 134 to 137
Winter: Mo 16.00–24.00; Tu–Th 11.00–24.00;
    Fr–Sa 11.00–01.00; Su 10.00–24.00
Summer: Su–Th 10.00–24.00; Fr–Sa 10.00–01.00

While the Alte Kolkshenke (above) may be the smallest pub in this guide, this near neighbour might well be the biggest. The Brauhaus is a large, redbrick brewpub with tower and chimney, its brewing kettles taking centre stage.

All the bus routes pass the S-Bahnhof, while from the U-Bahnhof, follow the same instructions as for the Alte Kolkshenke and look out for the tower and chimney.

Forgetting the fact its opening hours are of bewilderingly, almost Belgian complexity, this is a serious business, with several beer gardens, numerous spacious rooms including a special sports bar with big TV screen, plus a hotel.

The two beers brewed on site are Havelbräu, an unfiltered, fresh and lemony Helles that can be a little on the thin side, and **Brauhaus Spandau Spezialbier** (5.0–5.5%), which varies with the seasons and tends to be brown in colour. The most frequently found has a slightly burnt aroma, malty and vanilla tastes combining with sweet caramel. Despite its melange of tastes, it is also slightly thin.

Both beers are matured for two weeks in open fermenters, then finished for one week in the more usual (for Germany) closed, conical fermenters, giving them aspects of both lager and ale production. A draught Hefeweisse is also served, which is brewed here for the early summer.

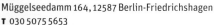

⑮ **Bräustübl** 🍺 ✖ ✿
Müggelseedamm 164, 12587 Berlin-Friedrichshagen
T 030 5075 5653
www.braeustuebl.de
🍴 Full menu from top-flight chefs
Ⓢ S3 (Friedrichshagen)
Ⓗ 60 & 61 (Müggelseedamm-Bölschestraße)
🕐 Daily 11.30 till late

This was once the brewery tap for the Berliner Bürgerbräu Brewery, known locally as BBB, but since being bought out by Radeberger Gruppe brewing has moved to BKS. The plans for the brewery site are uncertain but the Bräustübl has been rejuvenated by its new owners, who plan to restart brewing on a small scale inside BBB, and to serve the local Köpenick market. We hope they succeed.

Getting here involves some dedication. Come down the main staircase of the S-Bahnhof and turn right, crossing the main road (Fürstenwalder Damm) into Bölsche Straße, where you can catch the tram 20 metres down on the right. At the stop the pub is visible across the road at the T-junction.

Five ornate rooms await the adventurous toper, including a ballroom, a winter garden and an old taproom. Bräustübl serves the full range of BBB beers, including our choice of **Berliner Bürgerbräu Rotkehlchen** (5.3%), an export lager almost in the Vienna-style, reddish-brown in colour with a fresh malt flavour, finishing with a little sweetness. We would be recommending the more robust Bernauer Schwarzbier, but were incorrectly informed that this excellent Dunkel had been discontinued by BKS. Wrong. Last minute research reveals that it lives on. Other offerings are a spicy, dry, lemony Weissbier, with a hint of softness and vanilla, reminiscent of the Belgian brew Watou's Wit; and of course the classic Berliner Bürgerbräu Pils. There are also seven bottled options, including BBB Dunkles Hefeweisse and Berliner Weisse.

Just opposite Friedrichshagen S-Bahnhof at Furstenwalder Damm 484 is a local pub with real character called 'zur Stammkneipe', that also sells some BBB beers.

16   Brewbaker
Armenius Markthalle, Armenius Straße 2–4, 10551 Berlin
T 0177 694 0961
www.brewbaker.de
None at bar – linked restaurant
U9 (Turmstraße)
Sunday and holidays
Mo–Th 11.00–18.00; Fr 11.00–19.00; Sa 11.00–15.00.

Problems with lease issues mean that this wonderful brewpub, once found 'underneath the arches', moved premises in 2011 and became more of an open-air microbrewery and bar within the old Armenius Market Hall. Enter by the main gate in Armenius Strasse, navigate through all the food stalls and head for the far left-hand corner, where Brewbaker has risen anew in a much more spacious and interesting location than hitherto.

The old brewpub was famous for its innovative menu, featuring dishes such as Pork Cutlet with Mango-Plum Stew, Crème Brulee with Malzbier and Coq a la Biere. Happily, this legacy will survive with the 'Zunft Wirtschaft' restaurant also situated within the Armenius complex, that will serve Brewbaker beers and is open until midnight.

But the main interest here is of course the beer. Not least because the enthusiastic young owner-brewer (Michael Schwab) eschews the *Reinheitsgebot* to experiment with perhaps thirty different brews each year, many of them ales. In fact Michael has brewed 100 different beers since starting-up in 2005. Not spectacular by some standards, but for Germany, practically a miracle!

His regulars include **Brewbaker Pils** (5%), which is really bitter, dry and tart; and Brewbaker Weizen, also lemony tart but with some balancing softness. Regular beers at the new location will also be a Red Vienna-style Lager and an IPA. The ever-changing specials have featured Chilli Lager, which burns a hole in the back of your throat, Potato Stout, Pumpkin Ale, and the glorious Espresso Coffee Stout (pictured). And these are just the ones we have tasted on recent visits. What is actually available depends largely on potluck, and that is part of the fun. Other specials appearing at semi-regular intervals are Honey Porter and Brewers Blood Doppelbock. If you find out the latter is on, book a flight for the next day. All the beers are unfiltered, yet look as beautiful as they taste.

17 Brink's 🏛 🕒
Hasenheide 117, 10967 Berlin-Neukölln
T 030 622 6500
🍴 None
U U7 & U8 (Hermannsplatz)
🕐 Daily 09.00–01.00

This unassuming, basic corner local, easy to find, on the southwest corner of Hermannsplatz at the junction with Wissmann Straße, welcomes smokers and sports fans.

Several TV screens show any and all football matches, along with other less penetrable sports such as handball and cross-country skiing that Germans find watchable for reasons we have yet to grasp. A large, fake tree dominates the spacious back bar, with stuffed birds and other ephemera adorning its branches. There is a fantastic collection of old enamel advertising plaques, for beer, films, shipping lines, washing powders, Ovaltine and much else besides.

The beer range is well above average for this kind of corner local, with four pilsners, Sion Kölsch, and Köstritzer

Schwarzbier on draught and a seasonal draught sometimes on offer too.

Bottles run to just four, all Hefeweissens, including **Kloster Andechs Weissbier Hefetrub** (5.5%), a huge mouthful of yeasty banana, beautifully balanced with malt and citrus fruit in roughly equal measure. This pub is a meeting point for fans of Hertha BSC, whose relegation from the Bundesliga in 2010 left no representative from either Berlin or the former East Germany in top-flight German league football.

Clash

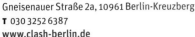
18 Clash
Gneisenauer Straße 2a, 10961 Berlin-Kreuzberg
T 030 3252 6387
www.clash-berlin.de
Limited
U6 & U7 (Mehringdamm)
Sunday
Mo–Fr 12.00 till late; Sa 18.30 till late

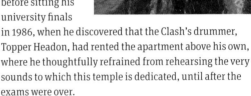

The author's personal choice, recalling the days, a few weeks before sitting his university finals in 1986, when he discovered that the Clash's drummer, Topper Headon, had rented the apartment above his own, where he thoughtfully refrained from rehearsing the very sounds to which this temple is dedicated, until after the exams were over.

Any ageing punk fan who enjoys a good beer will relish this anarchist dream, a sprawling tram shed of a building that is a shrine to Joe Strummer and his band, featuring skulls, skeletons and noise.

During the day, when live bands are unlikely to be performing, this can be difficult to find, hidden as it is in a courtyard down a dingy alley, close to the junction with Mehringdamm. If the door in front of you is shut, make a detour to the left into a run-down apartment block, then right and right again, through an unmarked door with an Astra beer sign above it.

Persistence is rewarded by the good and rare beers on offer here, including

the house beer **Waidbauer Pils** (4.7%) formerly from Stützhauser of Luisental, now brewed by Brauerei Gotha, both in Thüringen. This can be on the soapy side, but is quite drinkable and reminiscent of DDR-era draught beers – malty, moreish, slightly spiced but with minimal hop character. Other draught offerings include Flensburger Pils, and Louny Dunkel from the Czech Republic, plus a light Hefeweisse. Bottles include the splendid quartet of Augustiner Edelstoff, Rothaus Tannenzäpfle Pils, Astra Pils, and Augustiner Helles.

19 **Deponie #3** 🍺 ✕ ❋
Georgen Straße 5, 10117 Berlin-Mitte
T 030 2016 5740
www.Deponie3.de
🍴 Full menu with Berlin specialities
Ⓤ U6 (Friedrichstraße)
Ⓢ S3, S5, S7 & S75 (Friedrichstraße)
🕐 Mo–Fr 09.00 till late; Sa–Su 10.00 till late

Deponie is a wonderful old-style Berlin estaminet tucked
away underneath the railway arches between the
Freidrichstraße and Hackescher Markt S-Bahn stations.

The space used to be a tank depot for the DDR Volksarmee
– so there is plenty of it. There are two large main bars with
various nooks and crannies leading off, all cluttered with
ancient bric-a-brac. Despite that, this is a quiet, reflective pub,
like a *fin de siècle* Viennese coffee house during the day, yet
with the ever-present rumble of the trains moving overhead.
By night, Dr Jekyll transforms into Mr Hyde, as coach parties
of students arrive and turn the pub into hedonism central.

There is a small beer garden out the back, which is as
quiet a spot as any amidst the bustle of downtown Berlin.
The food menu is exhaustive, as are the portions. Breakfast
and ice cream seem to be specialities.

There are three draught German pilsners, plus
Böhmisches Dark & Light from the Czech Republic. These are
complemented by about eight bottles, including Rothaus
Tannenzäpfle Pils and their classic bestseller, **Augustiner
Helles** (5.2%), a crisp slightly sweet lager that finishes with
a little more bitterness than most Munich beers.
Such a pity it is not available on draught.

Dicke Wirtin

20 Dicke Wirtin
Carmer Straße 9, Am Savignyplatz, 10623 Berlin-Charlottenburg
T 030 312 4952
www.dicke-wirtin.de
Full menu with local specialities
S3, S5, S7 & S75 (Savingnyplatz)
Daily 12.00 till late

Just off the northeast corner of lively Savingnyplatz, visitors to the sister of the Dicker Wirt (below) are greeted by images of the Dicke Wirtin (fat hostess) herself – Roseanne Barr meets Nora Batty with a cigarette dangling from the corner of her mouth. This was Anna Stanscheck, an imposing lady famous for her big heart, monstrous stews and love for the students of the nearby Art School. The food menu remains hearty and classic Berlin.

To this day the pub claims proudly that it has always welcomed artists, authors, actors, and other *skurrilen*, a word that means exactly what you think it does.

The building is divided into three distinct areas, two bars at the front (one for smokers) and a restaurant to the rear. All rooms are crammed with assorted bric-a-brac, including maps and photos of old Berlin. The author fondly remembers spending all night drinking and playing bridge here just days after the Wall came down.

The excellent draught beer range includes Flensberger Pils, Schneider Weisse, Berliner Kindl Jubiläums Pils, Mönchshof Schwarzbier, and **König Pils** (4.9%); a pale golden pilsner from a huge brewery in Duisberg in the Ruhrgebiet. Clean, clear and fresh, it has a pronounced hop bitter finish. There is also a monthly special on draught and about 25 varieties of homemade schnapps dispensed from large bottles balanced above the bar. Bottled beers are limited to four versions of Schneider Weisse (all worth drinking) and Berliner Weisse.

Dicker Wirt

㉑ Dicker Wirt
Danckelmann Straße 43, 14059 Berlin-Charlottenburg
T 030 321 9942
www.dicker-wirt.de
Snacks only
U U2 (Sophie-Charlotte Platz)
S S41 & S42 (Westend)
Daily 15.00–04.00

In the brother of the Dicke Wirtin (above), 'mein host' is a large, beery, balding man (for Brits who remember the 1970s, think Arthur Mullard in *Yus My Dear*), with a fat cigar in his mouth.

Located just north of the junction with Knobelsdorff Straße, this is a large and surprisingly bare (for Berlin) pub, and much more of a serious drinking den than its sister. It can lack atmosphere during the afternoon, but comes alive at night with regular live music events. There is also a quiz night on Saturdays (20.00), for those who wish to put their German skills to the ultimate test.

The relatively extensive list of draught beers includes four pilsners, Erdinger Weißbier Hell, and Köstrizer Schwarzbier, along with the interesting and unique **Kiez Bier** (5%), specially brewed for the pub by some micro-brewery in Franconia, northern Bavaria, though we know not which. The six bottled beers including four different Hefeweissen (all good) from the Erdinger brewery.

Kiez means 'neighbourhood' in German, and the beer certainly has a homely quality. It's a light-golden, easy-drinking Helles with a smooth malty flavour, low carbonation and just enough hoppy kick to make it interesting. Slightly reminiscent of a DDR quaffing lager in fact. This pub now has a dark house beer as well called 'Kiez Schatten' ('shatten' means shadow) from the same brewery, which was too sweet for us to finish.

22 Endhorn ⊗ ⊕ ⊖

22 Endhorn ⊗ ⊕ ⊖

Belfort Straße 27, 10405 Berlin-Prenzlauerberg
T 030 440 8380

🍴 Good varied menu, summer only

Ⓤ U2 (Senefelderstraße)

⊗ Sunday

🕐 October to March: Mo–Sa 17.00–02.00
April to September: Mo–Sa 15.00–02.00

The Endhorn is another characterful corner pub in the trendy Prenzlauerberg district, but unique in that its winter guise (smoking, no food, cosy cellar bar) is completely different from its summer plumage, when it opens earlier and triples in size by colonising vast acres of pavement in all directions.
It bans indoor smoking in the summer because it provides a full menu.

It sits on the corner of Belfort Straße and Diedenhofer Straße. From the U-Bahnhof, go a few metres down Metzer Straße, turn left up Kollwitz Straße, and take the first right. Next door is a rare example of an un-renovated tenement building. Twenty years ago, much of the former

East Berlin looked like this.

Just north of Senefelderstraße U-Bahnhof is a Jewish cemetery that contains the graves of many prominent Berliners, including Samuel Bleichröder, founder of the Arnhold & S. Bleichröder bank, who was known as 'Bismarck's banker'. It moved to New York in 1937 for obvious reasons, and remains there to this day.

Flensburger Pils (4.9%) is a light, golden pilsner; clear, crisp, sharp and herbal, with a bitter finish. This is a fine example of a north German pilsner – it is difficult to get further north in Germany than Flensburg, which is right by the Danish border. Other draft beers are Wernesgrüner Pils, Franziskaner Hefeweisse and Köstritzer Schwarzbier.

Eschenbräu

㉓ Eschenbräu ✳ 🍺 🕐
Trift Straße 67, 13353 Berlin-Wedding
☎ 030 462 6837
www.eschenbraeu.de
🍴 Fresh-cooked Pretzels, cold Knackerwurst & Flammkuchen
Ⓤ U6 & U9 (Leopoldsplatz)
Ⓢ S41 & S42 (Wedding)
🕐 Daily 17.00 till late

This lovely, idiosyncratic brewpub, with its sideline in apple juice and fruit schnapps, is really difficult to find.

Walking west from the U-Bahnhof along Luxemburger Straße turn left (south) along Gentner Straße to its junction with Trift Straße. Keep straight on along a pedestrianised street and turn left after 30 metres underneath an apartment block into an open area, which is its beer garden! The brewery tap itself is to the right, down a small flight of steps.

The spacious courtyard beer garden is shaded and quiet. The small Bräukeller is a converted cellar and feels like a basic English pub.

These are amongst the finest beers of any brewpub in Berlin – fresh, tasty and unfiltered, and available in various takeaway containers. Three are available year-round; Dunkel, Weizen, and **Eschenbräu Pils** (5%), a robust, full flavoured, dry and spicy blond lager.

There is also a wonderful variety of rotating seasonal specials: Dunkler Bock from mid-February; Weddinator (a 7.8% doppelbock) in March; Rauchbier from mid-March; Hopfenblume from early April; a really special Maibock from 1st May; Bayrisch Hell from early June; Weizenbock in June; Roter Wedding (for the strong Communist roots of this district) from early July; Schwarze Molle from early August; Märzen from mid-September; Panke Gold (a 5.2% export lager) in October; Doppelhof (a 6.6% IPA) in November, and finally – deep breath – Alter Schwede from late November. From September 2011, a self-pressed 'Bio-Cider' will be served as well.

As this is the only Wedding pub in the guide, whilst up here we suggest you also take a look at 'Zum Magendoktor', a wonderfully unspoilt drinking den at Reinickendorfer Straße 111, right by the easterly exit of Wedding S-Bahnhof.

Felsenkeller

24 **Felsenkeller**
Akazien Straße 2, 10823 Berlin-Schöneberg
T 030 781 3447
Light snacks and the occasional stew
U U7 (Eisenacher Straße)
S S1 (Julius Leber Brücke)
Mo–Fr 16.00–02.00; Sa 12.00–02.00; Su 18.00–02.00

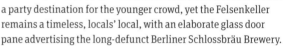

One delight of Berlin is that it keeps throwing up great, unspoilt locals where you least expect them. Akazien Straße is a party destination for the younger crowd, yet the Felsenkeller remains a timeless, locals' local, with an elaborate glass door pane advertising the long-defunct Berliner Schlossbräu Brewery.

Other features worth checking out are the shipping line posters, a stuffed seagull in mid-flight, the old food tin collection, an antique chocolate vending machine, and what looks like a Magritte painting (presumably a copy) by the window. The first bomb to fall on Berlin during 1939–45 destroyed the house next door, but the thousands that followed all miraculously missed this pub.

To get here, leave the U-Bahnhof heading east and Akazien Straße is the first on the right, by an enormous brick church.

The draught range is better than most, featuring among others Rothaus Tannenzäpfle Pils, König Pils, Jever Pils and from the Czech Republic Budweiser Budvar. All bottled options are Bavarian Hefeweissen, including the rare but excellent Unertl.

Also on draught is **Fürstenberg Pils** (4.8%) from Donaueschingen in Baden-Württemburg – the town's name referring to the fact that it is the official source of the river Danube. This is a lovely lemon-gold coloured lager with an ultra-smooth texture and balanced malty/hoppy flavours. Its brewers promote this as "one of the best beers in the World", with no 'probably' in sight.

Gambrinus

25 **Gambrinus**
Linien Straße 133, 10115 Berlin-Mitte
T 030 282 6043
www.gambrinus-berlin-mitte.de
Berlin-style
U U6 (Oranienburger Tor)
S S1, S2 & S25 (Oranienburger Straße)
H M1, M6 & 12 (Oranienburger Tor)
Mo–Sa 12.00–04.00; Su 15.00–04.00

Gambrinus is a small and lively pub in the heart of the Oranienburger Tor entertainment district, just north of the city centre.

It has two distinct areas, a real public bar at the front and a restaurant to the rear, though you can eat in the former and drink in the latter.

Over 100 years old, it was reconstructed in classic style by the DDR regime sometime around 1985. Note the ornate lamps above the bar, the chime clock collection and the numerous old photos and maps of Berlin. We like the hilarious DDR U-Bahn map from the 1950s, with the East proudly described as "Democratic Berlin", in contrast to the fascist West.

Local food specialities include a vast array of different schnitzels. This is also reputedly the first place to serve the famous Berlin Boulette back in 1896.

Draught beers include a Czech house beer called Gambrinus, now made by SAB-Miller, though our recommendation is **Engelhardt Pils** (5%). Originally from the now-closed Charlottenburg Brewery, it is a clear and bitter pilsner with a slightly thin finish, now brewed at BKS but retaining its Berlin heritage name and identity.

Other choices include the dry and bitter Jever Pils, Berliner Pils or

Köstritzer Schwarzbier. Bottled options include Berliner Weisse, three varieties of Schneider Weisse and Diebels Alt a dark brown malty ale from Düsseldorf, with a bitter finish.

Gasthaus Lentz

26 Gasthaus Lentz ✖ ✳

Stuttgarter Platz 20, 10627 Berlin-Charlottenburg

T 030 324 1619

www.gasthaus-lentz-berlin.de

🍽 Varied daily changing menu

Ⓤ U7 (Wilmersdorfer Straße)

Ⓢ S3, S5, S7 & S75 (Charlottenburg)

🕐 Daily 09.00–01.30

The Lentz is a light, cool establishment at the western end of Stuttgarter Platz, beyond the junction with Windschied Straße, on a pleasant corner of the square, attracting an arty, intellectual crowd throughout the day – whether they have jobs to go to we can only speculate.

Simple wooden tables adorn the single room, with bare white walls with minimal artwork and a red lino floor all coming together to create a unique atmosphere, where the only sounds are the rustle of newspapers and an occasional hiss from the coffee machine.

It is the sort of pub where your first impression of "let's stay just for one" gives way to lingering for hours. There are a few red-light establishments nearby though, so families tend to keep away. The annual Stuttifest (live music plus) takes place in June on the square and in surrounding streets.

The impressive draught beer list includes Jever Pils, Kloster Andechs Weissbier Hefetrub, Gaffel Kölsch, König Pils and Mönschof Kellerbier. Bottled beers include several wheat beers and **Kloster Andechs Spezial Hell** (5.8%), a classic example of the Spezial style of Bavarian lager that tends to be stronger and sweeter than the bitter pilsners of northern Germany. This one comes with some spice and just enough hop character to achieve a wonderful balance – definitely one from the very top drawer.

27 Gasthaus Wilhelm Hoeck 1892
Wilmersdorfer Straße 149, 10585 Berlin-Charlottenburg
T 030 341 8174
www.wilhelm-hoeck.de
🍴 Full menu with Berlin specialities
Ⓤ U7 (Bismarkstraße)
⊗ Sunday
🕐 Mo–Sa 11.30–01.00

We have concerns over the long-term viability of some pubs in this guide, but not this one. Even at opening time, there always seem to be a few locals getting the day's drinking off to a good start. Dark and atmospheric, this bar looks every bit as old as its name suggests.

Candlelight is needed even in daytime to observe the musty surrounds, including an enormous array of mysterious, odd-shaped spirit bottles stacked on shelves behind the bar. More bottles and some oak barrels are built into the back wall, while more pack an ornate glass cabinet high on the wall opposite the bar.

The Gasthaus is now two pubs for the price of one, since it opened a non-smoking restaurant next door, serving high-class German cuisine.

Draught beer is poured very slowly here, as it should be, so be prepared to wait, and consider ordering your second well before you've finished your first.

As well as our chosen beer there are Berliner Kindl Pils and Bock Dunkel (winter only), Märkisches Landmann Schwarzbier and Pilsner Urquell from the Czech Republic, plus five bottled Hefeweissen beers of varying sorts.

Bitburger Pils (4.8%) is claimed to be the first pilsner in the world brewed outside Bohemia and for a high volume production lager, the balance between floral, citrus hop and toasted malt is exceptional. Golden and moderately bitter, from the rural Hunsrück area of western Germany, it remains deservedly popular throughout Germany.

Just a hundred meters or so back along Zille Straße from here at number 22 is 'Rumpelkiste', another classic unspoilt local boozer that would be in the guide if the beer list extended beyond Schultheiss and a few bottles.

Georgbræu

28 **Georgbræu**
Spreeufer 4, 10178 Berlin-Mitte
T 030 242 42 44
www.georgbraeu.de
Full menu with Berlin specialities
U2 (Klosterstraße)
S3, S5, S7 & S75 (Alexanderplatz)
M4, M5 & M6 (Spandauer Straße/Marienkirche)
Daily from 10.00 (April to December), 12.00 (January to March)

When the Brauhaus in Rixdorf (above) ceased brewing, Georgbräu, opened in 1992, became the longest established brewpub in Berlin.

It takes its name from an elegant statue of St. George slaying the dragon, seen in the little square in front – though 'The Beer Emporium' might be more appropriate. Although the terrace shuts at 21.30 in summer and is closed in winter, we counted eight rooms inside and may have missed a few!

This place is vast and at times very lively, with a perfect riverside location and a sizeable, traditional beer garden on the terrace outside. If you can get a seat, this is a perfect spot to watch the tourist throngs pass by, either along the riverbank or in their flat-bottomed boats below.

Prominent copper brewing kettles sit behind the bar and produce two unfiltered beers, **Georg Pils** (5%), in light (Helles) and dark (Dunkles) varieties. They are brewed separately to different recipes but taste so surprisingly similar that it is easy to imagine that one is simply a caramelised incarnation of the other.

Be warned that the beers can be variable too. On one visit in 2009 both were insipid, lacked condition and even had a little sourness, while on another in November 2010 both were superb, with the Helles sporting a toffee-apple flavour and a fine, fruity-hop finish.

Glühwurm

㉙ Glühwurm ✪ ✪
Südwestkorso 69A, 12161 Berlin-Wilmersdorf
T 030 852 3067
www.gluehwurm-restaurant.de
Swabian (Baden-Württemberg) specialities
U U9 (Bundesplatz)
S S41, S42 & S45 (Mo–Fr only) (Bundesplatz)
Daily 16.00–24.00

On the corner with Görres Straße in a quiet residential district, the 'Glow Worm' is a Swabian pub and restaurant showcasing beer and food from the states of Baden-Württemburg and Bayern (Bavaria) in southern Germany.

Its décor is understated, with huge windows, a zigzag bar, wooden flooring and shelves behind the bar that contain wine glasses and not a lot else. There are smaller rooms off the main bar/restaurant area, with a small beer garden and seats on the pavement outside.

The menu has some interesting and rare Swabian wines on offer too – like those from Franconia in northern Bavaria, which rarely make it onto the international market as the locals drink them all themselves.

The draught beers have slightly less regional provenance. Although Rothaus Tannenzäpfle Pils is Swabian enough, Jever and Flensburger are north German while **Memminger Pils** (5.1%) is from the Bavarian side of the border with Baden-Württemburg. This last is creamy, earthy, robust and full-bodied – a bit like the Swabians as it happens – with just a hint of caramel.

There are seven bottled options too including a darker lager from Memminger, not dissimilar to a classic Vienna brew, albeit darker and hoppier, plus three wheat beers. All in all, an impressive array for what is primarily a local restaurant.

Gottlob

30 Gottlob
Akazien Straße 2, 10823 Berlin-Schöneberg
T 030 7870 8095
Breakfasts, pasta, salads, charcuterie & curry
U U7 (Eisenachstraße)
Mo–Th 09.00–01.00; Fr–Sa 09.00–02.00; Su 10.00–01.00

Gottlob is a trendy café-restaurant in a lively part of town, which offers excellent and varied food and some great beers. What's not to like?

Gottlob sometimes calls itself 'Move', though we have no idea why. The bar area is simple and bare with huge open windows, doubling in size when it spills out onto the pavement in both directions.

To get here, leave the U-Bahnhof by the easterly exit. You cannot miss the large brick church with its enormous spire – walk past the entrance to find the pub is on the other side of the street.

Somewhat out of place is the frieze around the ceiling that might be featured in *The Great Drawing Rooms of Europe*, if such a tome existed.

Combine a visit here with the Felsenkeller (above) and Leuchtturm (below).

The four draught beers are Bitburger Pils, Weihenstephan Hefeweisse Hell, Budweiser Budvar, and our chosen beer, **Bergisches Löwenpils** (4.8%). This is a light-golden ultra-smooth pilsner from

the Erzquell brewery in Bielstein, near Wiehl in Nordrhein-Westfalen, with some orange fruitiness in the finish, not unlike the Czech classic, Pilsner Urquell, in its full pomp, before its production was speeded up in pursuit of greater production.

There are some Hefeweissen offerings in bottles, and an excellent wine and spirits list to complete the picture.

Hackbarth

③① Hackbarth 🍺 🍴
August Straße 49a, 10119 Berlin-Mitte
T 030 282 7704
🍽 Eclectic menu and cakes
Ⓤ U8 (Weinmeisterstraße)
Ⓗ M1 & M8 (Rosenthaler Platz)
🕐 Daily 10.00 till late

Some interesting
and rare beers
await the visitor to
this über-trendy
back-street pub
with real Bohemian
character, which
often stays open till 03.00.

Even the bar shape is unusual, a giant
flatiron surrounded by lots of stools. The walls
are bare. There is a fantastic little snug area
at the back, ideal for a game of cards.

The varied menu offers tostadas, breakfast, vegetarian quiche, tortillas, soup and cheese
baguettes, not to mention the 'cakes of the day' written up on the chalkboard above the bar.
Both the snack and the main menu have something to suit all tastes, whilst smoking is only
permitted after 9pm.

The four draught beers are Zywiec
Pils (from Poland), Kloster Andechs
Spezial Hell, Streck's Hefeweisse and
Streck's Pils (4.8%), the latter also
branded Burgherren Pils, the pale-
straw coloured, dry, crisp and bitter-
hopped brew from the Streck brewery
in the village of Ostheim vor der Rhön
in Franconia, northern Bavaria.

There is a good bottled range as
well, including two more Streck beers
and from the same brewery Ostheimer
Dunkel, which combines burnt notes
with some bitterness. Beyond beer
the drinks menu is strong on wine
and spirits, and has 20 different
cocktails and 14 different teas.

32 Hax'nhaus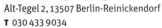

Alt-Tegel 2, 13507 Berlin-Reinickendorf

T 030 433 9034

www.haxnhaus.de

Full menu with a Bavarian hint

U U6 (Alt-Tegel)

S S25 (Tegel)

Daily 10.00–24.00

The Hax'nhaus is a rustic and authentic recreation of a Bavarian village tavern, out in the wilds of Tegel, complete with stone floor, hunting trophies and stripped pine – lots of stripped pine.

In fact you get two Hax'nhauser for the price of one – an identikit overspill pub exists upstairs, along with a small, covered terrace for smokers. The beer garden at the front sits in a busy pedestrianised street and is a pleasant place to recover from lunch with a litre jug (or *Maß*) of beer.

Draught beers are Veltins Pils, Augustiner Helles, Köstritzer Schwarzbier, and **Maisel's Weisse Original** (5.2%), a darkish, mid-brown Weisse from Bayreuth in Bavaria (of Richard Wagner fame). It yeasty and dry, with a touch of toffee, banana and spice in the finish. The two bottled beers are Berliner Weisse and Maisel's Hefeweisse Dunkel.

The varied food menu delivers substantial portions of classic Bavarian fare, including the massive *Schweinhaxe*, which as the pub name suggests is their signature dish. If you ever find yourself out here on a Sunday morning, they do a good Sunday brunch (09.00–12.00).

The smaller, more basic Dorf Krug, next door, has five draught beers and plenty of Bayern Munich football-related stuff.

Hell oder Dunkel

㉝ Hell oder Dunkel 🍴 ❌ ❄

Laubacher Straße 28, 14197 Berlin-Wilmersdorf

T 030 8973 3620

www.helloderdunkel.de

🍴 Burger-centric

Ⓤ U9 (Bundesplatz)

Ⓢ S41, S42 & S45 (Mo–Fr only) (Bundesplatz)

🚌 101 (Laubacher Straße/Vartziner Straße)

🕐 Mo–Sa 15.00 till late; Su 13.00 till late

The main north-south urban motorway actually goes east-west near here, while the ring S-Bahn railway pass within metres of this pub. Despite this the atmosphere here at the 'Light or Dark' is one of seclusion and peace.

The pub is divided into three small bars with a pleasant little beer garden at the front and to the side. All have an odd feature in that small areas of brickwork have been left exposed beneath the plaster, like splodges of brown sauce on a white tablecloth. The TV in the main bar shows live football.

The substantial and varied menu includes about ten different sorts of burger, plus Münchener Weisswurst and roast goose.

The house beers here are indeed light or dark, being Helles and Spezial from Bräuhaus Spandau (above). Oddly, they often taste a little better here than at the brewery itself. **Brauhaus Spandau Havelbräu Hell** (5.2%) is an unfiltered, chewy, yeasty, quaffing beer that manages to be both mild and bitter at the same time.

Other beers include Krombacher Pils, Berliner Pils, and Schöfferhoffen Grapefruit (don't ask). About ten bottled beers are also available, along with a substantial spirits and cocktails list – we have not tried their 'Flying Kangaroo'. We dare you.

Hopfingerbräu

Hopfingerbräu ✖ ✱
Im Hauptbahnhof, Europaplatz 1, 10557 Berlin-Mitte
T 030 2062 4624
www.hopfingerbraeu-berlin.de
Berlin and Bavarian specialities
U55 (Hauptbahnhof)
S3, S5, S7 & S75 (Hauptbahnhof)
Daily 11.00–23.00

Hopfingerbräu is a substantial 'brewpub' within the amazing modernist Hauptbahnhof complex – though it has never brewed on the premises. Nevertheless, this is an excellent place to while away an hour before catching a train. It is also the start-point for our historical pub crawl (see page 11).

The extraordinary new main railway station has to be seen as a destination in its own right. This place is towards the northern entrance, one floor beneath the east-west tracks and three above the north-south lines.

A sizeable beer garden terrace directly overlooks an open space near to the "death strip" behind the Berlin Wall. It features a large horse-like mechanical sculpture that we believe doubles as a clock.

The sole house beer is the excellent Hofbräu Weisse, brewed at the Lindenbrau brewpub at the Sony Centre in Potsdamer Platz (below). The ornate brass brewing kit around and behind the bar is just for show and storage space.

Other draught beers are Fürsten Pils and **Altbairisch Dunkel** (5.3%), both of which come from their *Patronanzbrauerie* (patron's brewery) at Traunstein in Bavaria. This deep-brown beer has a burnt chocolate aroma, develops sweetish honey and syrup flavours but finishing fresh, dry and sharp. It makes a perfect start to, or recovery from, a long train journey.

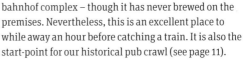

59

35 Hops & Barley 🍺 ⏰ 🍴 ☕

Wuhlisch Straße 22, 10345 Berlin-Friedrichshain

T 030 2936 7534

www.hopsandbarley-berlin.de

🍴 Bread snacks and sausage

Ⓤ U5 (Samariterstraße)

Ⓢ S3, S5, S7 & S75 (Warschauer Straße)

Ⓗ M13 (Wühlisch Straße/Gärtner Straße)

🕐 Mo–Fr 17.00–02.00; Sa–Su 15.00–02.00

Founded in February 2008 in the premises of an old butchers shop, and a magnificent addition to the Berlin beer scene, this new-wave brewpub attracts quite a young crowd. It even has a bargain guest room above the brewery, sleeping up to six.

The entrance is into a public bar that contains a tiny Braxonia two-barrel kit brewery, framed by some classic Portuguese *azulejo* tiles. It is the same as at Marcus Brau (below) and would be a contender for the 'smallest brewery in Germany' award, except that it is rarely used nowadays. A much larger, more practical brewhouse is located around the back.

The much larger back room is for smokers. Both areas have a basic, earthy quality with original features. Kimber, the enormous and loveable pub dog is another of these.

Football is shown on two big screens. Quality snacks are prepared with homemade and filling 'Treberbrot' bread. Add ham, cheese, salami, bockwurst and knackerwurst. They also commission and serve a good, draught medium-dry cider.

The four excellent house brews on tap are all proudly labelled 'bio', meaning they must be brewed using organic grain only and with no additives. There are three regulars plus a seasonal special – a delicious, clear, reddish Maibock on our

last visit. The regular Dunkel is a deep brown malty beer that is served a little too cold. The Weisse is robust, spicy and tart, not dissimilar to the **Hops & Barley Bio Pilsner** (4.8%), a very sharp, bitter and citric pilsner, or, described by it brewer as: "A beer with guts."

zur Kleinen Markthalle
Legiendamm 32, 10969 Berlin-Kreuzberg
T 030 614 2356
www.zur-kleinen-markthalle.de
Full menu
U8 (Moritzplatz)
Mo–Sa from 16.00; Su from 12.00

'On the Small Market Hall' is a dark, atmospheric pub occupying the surviving corner (possibly the poultry section) of a once-thriving 19th Century market, close to the route of the Wall.

This is the real Berlin, where the tables are not perpetually *reserviert* (reserved). The main bar – or market hall – has a thick, oak-beamed ceiling and is stuffed with reminders of its former use, including many old, evocative photos of a long-since-vanished Berlin.

The quiet and shaded beer garden at the front is only usually open in summer. Good food is served all day with gorgeous roast chicken being the loosely themed house speciality.

The draught beer selection here is well above average, with Schultheiss, Krombacher, Jever and König pilsners, Schneider Weisse Hefedunkel, and our choice, **Kulmbacher Mönchshof Schwarzbier** (4.9%), a splendid roasted malt, abbey-style beer with liquorice and bitterness in its finish – not unlike Fullers London Porter, though marginally stronger. Bottled beers include Schneider Weisse and Berliner Weisse.

The wine, schnapps and single-malt whiskies are also worth checking out too.

For a complete contrast, we dare you to visit 'Rota Rosa' just round the corner in Adelbert Straße 9, just about the roughest dive we have visited in all Berlin.

Lange Nacht

37 Lange Nacht 🍺 🚭
Weise Straße 8, 12049 Berlin-Neukölln
T 030 6272 1015
www.lange-nacht.com
🍴 Snacks only
U U8 (Boddingstraße)
🕐 Daily 18.00–03.00

On the corner of Selchower Straße, the 'Long Night' is another basic backstreet corner boozer for night owls, as its name suggests. In summer, seats and tables spill out onto the pavement and there is a constant backdrop of funk and soul music. The roll-up TV screen shows Bundesliga matches.

The big difference with this one is that it sells a rare beer, **Rollberg Hell** (5%), from a new microbrewery set up within the former Kindl brewery, just up the hill from here.

This micro also produces a Rotbier and a Hefeweissen, both also excellent. About thirty outlets are supplied, each vetted by the punk fan brewer. This pub was considered anarchic and scruffy enough to qualify. He is also trying to get his beer into Clash (above), when a tap becomes available.

This is a highly drinkable, unfiltered yet clear light-golden brew with a fresh-mown grass aroma and vanilla smoothness in the taste, balanced by spicy lemon bitterness. The low carbonation level suggests it may even be top-fermented.

Other draught choices are Jever Pils, Veltins Pils and Erdinger Weißbier Hell, along with about nine bottled options.

38 Latichte (Altberliner Schnappshaus)

Alt-Reinickendorf 29a, 13407 Berlin-Reinickendorf

T 030 495 2168

Classic German

U8 (Paracelus Bad)

S25 (Alt Reinickendorf)

Sunday

Mo–Sa 16.00–24.00

This beautiful, unspoilt village pub is some way out of the centre but still within the city, and well worth the trek.

Be aware that four streets are clustered together here, all called Alt Reinickendorf and that no. 29 has units that run from 'a' to 'h', which cover two of these.

Coming out of the U-Bahn head further out of town and then turn right at Roedern Allee, a main road, before turning right again into Alt Reinickendorf. Taking the next left the pub should be on your left. From the S-Bahn turn left out of the station, walk along the path through the woods and you should spot the pub on your right.

The menu is really impressive here, with 12 different types of schnitzel including an XXL that must be seen to be believed. Several dishes feature homemade *Käsespatzel*, a sort of pasta made with sourdough and flavoured with cheese, a dish rarely seen outside its home region of Baden-Württemberg.

Draught beers are Warsteiner Pils, Jarosover Pils, a Czech beer called Schwartz, and **Isenbeck Pils** (4.8%) a very pleasant, soft, creamy and dryish pilsner from Paderborn in Nordrhein-Westphalia. Bottles are restricted to three Hefeweissen beers from Erdinger and Berliner Weisse.

For a change, the schnapps list really is as impressive as the pub name suggests, with seven Berlin specialities. Try the fairly sweet but very nutty Walnut Schnapps or, for a sharper choice, Kümmel straight from the fridge.

On the way back to town, why not stop off at S-Bahnhof Nervenklinik and have a chaser in the 'S-Bahn Stubchen', a great little time-warp local serving Shultheiss Pils and not much else.

39 zum Liebarzt 🍺 ✖ 🍴
Conrad-Blenkle Straße 61, 10407 Berlin-Prenzlauerberg
T 030 4737 8308
🍴 Ever-changing chalkboard menu
Ⓢ S8, S9, S41 & S42 (Landsberger Allee)
Ⓗ M10 (Landsberger Allee/Petersburger Straße)
🕐 Daily 16.00–02.00

Zum Liebarzt is yet another great little East Berlin *ecke* (or corner tavern) at the junction with Cothenius Straße.

It has excellent food but only a limited draught beer selection. Unusually for Berlin, smoking seems to be allowed while eating – at least many locals here partake of both at the same time. This seems odd for a pub called 'The Beloved Doctor' and one wonders whether Cothenius, physician to the court of Frederick the Great, would approve. His portrait, which hangs prominently between two windows, suggests he may have enjoyed a jar or three himself.

This is the nearest pub in this guide to the BKS brewery, and thus is an obvious place to drink **Berliner Pils** (5%), a Berlin institution and the city's most popular beer. This is the driest and most bitter of the beers coming out of BKS and is consistently good.

Its two other draught beers are both from the Czech Republic – Jarosover Pils and Bruno, the latter being a sweetish, choco-malt Schwarz beer. The bottled beer selection is more impressive, with eleven to choose from including four Hefeweissen beers.

While you're in the area, make sure to visit the nearby pub 'Lisa', just down Cothenius Straße towards the main road – a great little basic boozer with Hohenthanner beers.

Lemke am Hackescher Markt

Lemke am Hackescher Markt
S-Bahnbogen 143, Dircksen Straße, 10178 Berlin-Mitte
T 030 24 72 87 27
www.brauerei-lemke.de
Full menu
S3, S5, S7 & S75 (Hackescher Markt)
Daily 12.00–02.00

More formally referred to as Lemkes Spezialitätenbrauerei, or simply Brauhaus Lemke, this sprawling, comfortable and atmospheric brewpub is underneath the railway arches just west of Alexanderplatz, close to the bustling Hackescher Markt.

There are two distinct sections, each under a separate arch, one featuring the bar and the other the brewing kit. The brewing area features a raised area fitted out with comfortable leather sofas, rather than the traditional long wooden tables and chairs elsewhere – perfect for relaxation after a busy day of sightseeing. There is a small beer garden and covered smoking area outside.

The food is extensive, classy and very good but we are here for the beer.

The four draught brews extend beyond the confines of Helles and Dunkles so prevalent throughout Germany. They usually include an interesting seasonal offering, such as a light, saison-style Kupfer in summer or a darker, stronger, higher malt Bock or Zwickelbier in winter. This last is a young or 'green' beer, fresh but with a nutty dryness that develops a bitter-orange finish.

The seasonal beers complement the regular Pils, Original, and **Brauhaus Lemke Weisse** (5%), which is mid-copper brown in colour, yeasty with floral hop aromas and a hint of banana.

Lemke am Schloß

41 **Lemke am Schloß**
Luisenplatz 1, 10585 Berlin-Charlottenburg
T 030 3087 8979
www.brauhaus-lemke.de
Full menu
U U7 (Richard Wagner Platz)
S S41 & S42 (Westend)
BUS M45 & 109 (Luisenplatz)
Fr–Sa 11.00–02.00; Su–Th 11.00–01.00

Formerly the Luisenbrau, this substantial, smart
brewpub was taken over by Lemke several years ago
and now brews their full beer range on an equal footing
with the original downtown Lemke (above).

   The main bar area sprawls around the central counter,
giving the impression and feel of multiple rooms. The much
older-looking restaurant area down a small flight of steps
to the right as you enter is usually
reserved for parties, we think.

   There is a great view of the
Charlottenburg Palace from both inside
the bar and the outside pavement
seating at the front. The palace, an
enormous, early 18th Century, Baroque
and Rococo edifice was commissioned
for Sophie-Charlotte, wife of Friedrich
III, the Hohenzollern soldier-king
who ruled Prussia at the time.

   His son and successor, Frederick
the Great, hated his ultra-strict father
and abandoned Charlottenburg
for the smaller and more intimate
Sanssouci Palace in Potsdam.

   The draught beer range is as at
Lemke (above) – even the seasonal
specials are common to both. **Brauhaus
Lemke Original** (5.5%) is arguably the
best of the lot – a dark, chestnut-malty
brew with roast and burnt notes,
finishing with a little restrained
bitterness. Similar to a good English
Old Ale in fact. Difficult at first but
persevere and you should start to get it.

42 **zur Letzten Instanz**
Waisen Straße 14–16, 10179 Berlin-Mitte
T 030 242 5528
www.zurletzteninstanz.de
Classy and expensive
U U2 (Klosterstraße)
S S3, S5, S7 & S75 (Alexanderplatz)
Mo–Sa 12.00–01.00; Su 12.00–23.00

Dating from 1621, this is a contender for the title of Berlin's oldest pub and as zum Nußbaum (below) was rebuilt after the war, it probably has the better claim.

Inside are several small rooms, mostly devoted to eating, with blackened wood-panelled walls and an ancient, working stove. Napoleon allegedly stopped for a drink here on his way to Moscow – though he was probably

more in need of one on the way back. The massive, elaborate chair in which he is said to have sat makes up one side of the *Stammtisch,* the table for regulars only. Every German pub has one of these and you may have no problem sitting at it provided you are happy to chat with everyone else.

To avoid being a victim of the *reserviert* curse become a perpetrator – book ahead if you want to eat here. We have seen people turned away from having a beer when the place

was almost empty, just because of diners on a promise.

Beers are unfortunately limited to BKS and include Berliner and Kindl Jubiläums Pils plus Märkishes Landmann Schwarz. **Schultheiss Pils** (5%) is an iconic Berlin brew, pale gold with grapefruit tartness and sweetish vanilla. It is not far off the bitterness of Berliner Pils.

All are served from fonts that look as if they date from 1621 too. In contrast the toilet doors definitely do not. These alone are worth the visit.

Leuchturm

43 Leuchturm
Crelle Straße 41, 10827 Berlin-Schöneberg
T 030 781 8519
www.leuchturm-kneipe.de
Snacks only
U U7 (Kleistpark)
S S1 (Julius Leber Brücke)
Summer: Mo–Fr 16.00–03.00; Sa 18.00–03.00; Su 16.00–03.00
Winter: Mo–Fr 18.00–03.00; Sa 20.00–03.00; Su 18.00–01.00.

The 'Lighthouse' is another atmospheric, unspoilt backstreet boozer, aimed at the night-time trade. The interior dates from 1896, but must have been brought in from elsewhere, as the pub has only been here since 1964!

This is practically an art gallery, and an ideal setting for the literary round-table founded here in 1994. A small back room contains a table-footy machine, which might have been the inspiration behind "The Goalkeepers Fear of the Penalty", one of Berlin-based film director Wim Wenders' more famous films. He is said to be a regular. Combine a visit here with a foray across the main road (Potsdamer Straße) to Felsenkeller and Gottlob (above) in nearby Akasien Straße.

An excellent draught beer selection includes Jever, Bitburger, Berliner and Hohenthanner Schloßpils, plus the rarer Jever Schwarzbier. It is a good place to drink **Warsteiner Premium Verum** (4.8%), a pale straw-lemon coloured, smooth, lightly bitter beer with some peppery spice.

The bottled range is not a patch on the draught but does include the acceptable-but-not-outstanding Schöfferhofer Hefeweisse in three forms: Helles, Dunkel and Kristal. Food stretches as far as Berliner Boulette, salads and sausage.

Lindenbräu

44 Lindenbräu

Sony Centre, Bellevue Straße 3–5, 10785 Berlin-Tiergaten

T 030 2575 1280

www.lindenbraeu-berlin.de

Full menu

U U2 (Potsdamer Platz)

S S1, S2 & S25 (Potsdamer Platz)

Su–Th 11.00–01.00; Fr & Sa 11.00–02.30

Lindenbräu (or Limes' Brew) is one of the biggest of Berlin's many brewpubs, sprawling over three stories of the imposing Sony Centre, without counting the terrace and beer garden.

Sat in an entire mini city of ultra-modern buildings, each designed by a different globally renowned architect, the Sony Centre is the work of legendary Italian designer Renzo Piano and arguably the most impressive of all. Piano's previous works included the Pompidou Centre in Paris.

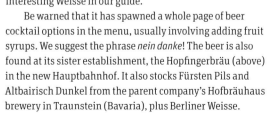

The development occupies land that straddled the Berlin Wall until 1989, around Potsdamer Platz and Leipziger Platz, and plenty of Cold War remnants survive, including whole slabs of the Wall itself, still in their original position.

Just one beer is brewed here – in the World's only silver-plated brew kettle! **Lindenbräu Hofbräu-Weiße** (5%) is lemony, refreshing and unfiltered, nicely balancing vanilla smoothness from the malt, banana from the yeast and lemon from the hops.

It is possibly the most accomplished and certainly the most interesting Weisse in our guide.

Be warned that it has spawned a whole page of beer cocktail options in the menu, usually involving adding fruit syrups. We suggest the phrase *nein danke*! The beer is also found at its sister establishment, the Hopfingerbräu (above) in the new Hauptbahnhof. It also stocks Fürsten Pils and Altbairisch Dunkel from the parent company's Hofbräuhaus brewery in Traunstein (Bavaria), plus Berliner Weisse.

Marcus Bräu

45 Marcus Bräu
Munz Straße 1–3, 10178 Berlin-Mitte
T 030 247 69 85
www.marcus-braeu.de
Limited menu, with Flammkuchen and chalkboard specials
U U8 (Weinmeisterstraße)
S S3, S5, S7 & S75 (Alexanderplatz)
Mo–Fr 11.00–03.00; Sa–Su 16.00–03.00

Alternatively known as Bräuhaus Alexanderplatz and
Microbrauerei Barkowsky, the Marcus is a small brewpub
with bags of character, claiming to contain the smallest
commercial brewing plant in the world, though we think we
have seen others the same size in Berlin. Maybe the claim has
something to do with it being built into the back of the bar.

There is plenty here to keep the casual bric-a-brac
browser amused. Look out for the large notice boards bearing
words of wisdom, such as Martin Luther's: "We are all beggars
and thieves". Another says: "God protects this house from
emergencies and fire, but not from the taxman or the town
planning department". A third sports: "Customers can be
just about anybody. For proof, take a look at yourself!"

Its late opening makes it a great place for a 'last of
the evening' but be warned that if punters are thin on the
ground it may close early. For the foolhardy, the three house
schnapps can be ordered by the metre (as can the beer).

Smoking is normally only allowed at the bar,
but is tolerated everywhere once the food stops
at midnight. Flammkuchen (not far off pizza but
originally from the Alsace) are the speciality.

Although they have a standard filtered pilsner from
Veltins brewery in Duisberg their own kit produces unfiltered
pilsner and dunkel to a remarkably high standard.
Our choice has to be the pale-coloured, lemony, tart and
bitter **Marcus Bräu Pils** (5%). The Dunkel is smooth,
rich and creamy with both coffee and chocolate flavours.

*Just a few meters further up Munz Strasse at number 23 is
'Alt Berlin', a real smoker's paradise that opens, and shuts, late.
Non-smokers will need masks and oxygen tanks in here.*

46 Maria & Josef
Hans-Sachs Straße 5, 12205 Berlin-Zehlendorf
T 030 257 62851
www.mariaundjosef.com
Full menu with Bavarian bias
S1 (Lichterfelde West)
Mo–Fr 13.00–24.00; Sa–Su 12.00–24.00 or later

Time to head out of town. The 'Mary & Joseph' is a charming Bavarian-themed pub and beer garden out in the south-western suburbs, which serves excellent beer and super food at pleasingly low prices.

The beer garden entrance is a hop skip and jump from the S-Bahn station. From the outbound platform turn right, then left, go up the stairs and the garden should be just ahead. It can seat around 400, and although quiet on weekday lunchtimes gets much busier on fine summer evenings and at weekends.

The small two-roomed pub is well stocked with logs for winter evenings.

"A beer" here is a half litre – ask for 'large' and a litre Maß of Oktoberfest fame will arrive. On our last visit, this helped to wash down baby back ribs with a garlic and paprika tomato sauce, served with a lentil and orange salad. Perfect.

There are six draught brews, plus three light or low-alcohol, all from the famous Weihenstephan brewery in Freising, Bavaria, which can track its roots from the 11th

Century to the extent that it is officially the world's oldest surviving brewery. And it's all good stuff.

Its Hefeweisse Hell is the world-renowned wheat beer but there are also Hefeweisse Dunkel, Kristallweissbier, a tart, grapefruity Helles called Original, Tradition Dunkel and **Weihenstephaner Pils** (5.1%). This clear, light, golden and beautifully balanced beer mixes vanilla-smooth malt with a refined hop bitter finish.

47 Max und Moritz
Oranien Straße 162, 10969 Berlin-Kreuzberg
T 030 695 15 911
www.maxundmoritzberlin.de
Full menu
U U8 (Moritzplatz)
Daily 17.00 till late

A Berlin institution named after a famous pair of cheeky storybook children immortalised by Wilhelm Busch in 1903.

There is a slightly faded elegance to the place – all old oak and green enamel tiles – as if built for grander times. It comes closer to capturing the decadence of end-of-Weimar Berlin, of Christopher Isherwood and Sally Bowles, than anywhere else we know.

This Tardis of a pub has bags of character and just seems to go on and on. The large room at the back has a stage for live music and cabaret. Upstairs is a library, a private dining room, and even a small hotel.

The menu is packed with old Berlin specials. How about 'salted and pickled pork foot with pickled cabbage, mustard and potatoes'? Or 'braised, seasoned meatballs with a light cream caper sauce, boiled potatoes and salad'. Flammkuchen and lamb stew also feature as house specialities.

The Kreuzberger Molle house beer is from the Südstern microbrewery (below) and the same as unfiltered spicy and bitter Schoppe Brau Helles, simply re-badged for this pub. Our choice is **Barre Bräu Pils** (4.8%), a rare find from Lübbecke in eastern Westphalia, a well-balanced, crystal clear, golden pilsner, with some apple-hop fruitiness. Other draughts include Kapuziner Hefeweisse Hell and Mönchshof Schwarzbier, with Kulmbacher Premium Pils, Berliner Weisse and two more Kapuziner beers in bottle.

48 Metzer Eck
Metzer Straße 33, 10405 Berlin-Prenzlauerberg
T 030 442 76 56
www.metzer-eck.de
Classic Berlin, plus specials
U2 (Senefelderplatz)
Mo–Fr 16.00–01.00; Sa–Su 18.00–01.00

Dating from 1913, Metzer Eck is an old family-run East Berlin corner bar renovated to the sort of full *fin de siècle* elegance that was still being created before the First War. A pleasant beer garden out on the street is added in summer.

Its several small rooms rise upwards and backwards from the tiny bar, prompting the respected local newspaper, the *Berliner Zeitung* to call this "probably the best corner pub in the city". Best or not, it is certainly up there.

The food menu is strong on soups and stews, with Eisbein (boiled pork knuckle) specials in winter on Friday and Saturday.

In addition to the two pilsners the draught beers here include a mystery Hausmarke Schwarzbier (or house black beer), a dark ruby-coloured, smooth, coffee-roast dry stout-like brew with a hint of dry fruit, which we might have featured as our recommended brew had the staff not been convincingly ignorant of who brews it or where. It is served in a tall anonymous Kamphenkel glass made by a large brewing industry supply firm.

So we will plump for **Erdinger Kristall** (5.3%), the refreshing but lightish, soft and yeasty-but-filtered Weisse that might even be improved by the addition of a slice of lemon.

[Editor's note: we know the marketing guy who first put the slice of lime in the neck of that Latin American non-entity of a beer. He thought the nitwit market would assume it was the original for lager 'n' lime.]

49 Mittmann's 🍺 ✗
Runge-Ecke, Brucken Straße, 10179 Berlin-Mitte
T 030 279 3502
www.mittmanns.de
🍴 German, with fish a speciality
Ⓤ U8 (Jannowitzbrucke)
Ⓢ S3, S5, S7 & S75 (Jannowitzbrucke)
⊗ Sunday
🕐 Mo–Fr 11.30 till late; Sa 17.00 till late

Cosy little Mittmann's is on the corner of Runge Straße and Brucken Straße, just over the bridge from the S-Bahnhof. It claims to be over one hundred years old and also one of the top 400 cafés in Germany – an assertion that seems somewhat difficult to disprove.

It is certainly one of the best 80 in Berlin and picks itself as a destination for lovers of beer memorabilia and other assorted bric-a-brac, studiously collected from around the world. Look out for the Continental Tyres advert – we never knew they made beer as well!

As with most corner pubs in the city, seating spills out onto the pavement in fine weather and being situated just down the street from the Chinese Embassy, it makes a great place to watch people with a wide variety of grievances.

Among five reasonably well-known draught beers is **Gaffel Kölsch** (4.8%) one of the best of the golden-coloured, sharp, fresh and bitter ales made exclusively in Köln (Cologne), according to an official EU designation. Here it is served as it should be, in a small 20cl straight glasses with a dense, lasting *schaum* (or head). If they start bringing a fresh glass every time you are about to finish, place a beer mat on top of the glass.

50 Mommsen-Eck (Haus der 100 Biere)
Mommsen Straße 45, 10629 Berlin-Charlottenburg
T 030 324 2580
www.mommsen-eck.de

Extensive menu that varies through the day
U7 (Wilmersdorfer Straße)
S3, S5, S7 & S75 (Charlottenburg)
Daily 09.00 till late

On the corner of Mommsen Straße and Wilmersdorfer Straße, opposite the Bayern-Brunnen, a fountain from the era of Bismark and Queen Victoria, the Mommsen Eck has been a bar for over a century.

This place is vast, seating several hundred people in a large number of rooms and out in the lovely beer garden, enabling it to maintain a convivial atmosphere. Look up anywhere inside and you will see serried ranks of beer bottles, most of them full, lined up as if for inspection.

As the bar's sub-title suggests, they do stock a hundred beers but that is just the bottles. There are a further fifteen on tap. While a number are at the duller more international end of the spectrum there are enough really great brews to keep even the most jaded or discerning suds-supper happy.

The choices are too numerous to list, but amongst the bottles check out these four, every one a classic: König Ludwig Vollbier, Paulaner Salvator, Augustiner Edelstoff and Aecht Schlenkerla Rauchbier Märzen, the last a favourite of the author and described in the next entry.

Amongst the draught offerings, our pick is **Kloster Andechs Doppelbock Dunkel** (7%), a real Christmas pudding of a beer, strong with complex nutty and dried fruit flavours, especially dates. Sweetish to begin with, it is balanced by some hop bitterness in the finish.

51 Mommseneck am Potsdamer Platz ✗ ❀
Alte Potsdamer Straße 1, 10785 Berlin-Mitte
T 030 2529 6635
www.mommseneck.de
🍴 Full menu, with Berlin specialities
Ⓤ U2 (Potsdamer Platz)
Ⓢ S1, S2 & S25 (Potsdamer Platz)
🕐 Daily 11.00–01.00 (closing time can vary)

This is the sister-pub to the previous entry, and also features well over 100 beers. This is a huge, modern dining pub with a log fire in winter and a pleasant beer garden for summer.

A neon bicycle sculpture adorns the square pond just outside, while all around is a futuristic cityscape where dozens of leading international architects were given a free rein to let rip in what was formerly a dead area straddling the Wall.

Although the proportion of duffers lurking in the extensive bottled range is slightly higher here, of the ten draughts on offer, the bulk are worth drinking. These include König Ludwig Dunkel, Bitburger Pils, Weihenstephan Hefeweisse Hell and Köstritzer Schwarzbier.

Our choice comes from among the bottles and is the amazing and unique **Aecht Schlenkerla Rauchbier Märzen** (5.1%), a dark reddish-brown beer with an intense smoked aroma and the taste of smoky bacon crisps that lingers in the mouth alongside a refreshing hop bitterness that lasts long after the glass is empty.

Smoked beers are a tradition of Bamberg in the Franconia region of northern Bavaria, where this one is brewed. It is a beautiful city, much of which has been designated a UNESCO World Heritage site, and has no fewer than ten breweries.

Some people understand this beer immediately while others are put off by its oddness. After extensive research we have concluded that the third or fourth always tastes better than the first, so persevere.

Mutter Hoppe

Mutter Hoppe

Rathaus Straße 21, 10178 Berlin-Mitte

T 030 241 5625

www.mutterhoppe.de

Huge range of German and Berlin classics

U U2 (Klosterstraße)

S S3, S5, S7 & S75 (Alexanderplatz)

H M4, M5 & M6 (Spandauer Straße/Marienkirche)

Daily 11.30 till late

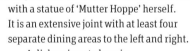

Next door to the Alt Berliner Weissbierstube (above) is 'Mother Hops', a cellar bar that is subdued and gloomy by day, but livens up at night, especially at weekends when live music plays.

The bar is entered down a spiral staircase decorated with old Berlin prints, which opens into an entrance lobby decorated

with a statue of 'Mutter Hoppe' herself. It is an extensive joint with at least four separate dining areas to the left and right.

A dish unique to here is *Hugenottenpfanne*, a massive frying pan full of marinated pork fillets, potato dumplings, fried eggs, beans, and parsley mushrooms. Alternatively, groups of ten or more can put in an advance order for *Die Spanferkel-Runde*, or whole roast pig if you want the simple version.

Draught beers are Radeberger Pils, Märkisches Landmann Schwarzbier, Erdinger Hefeweissen Hell, and **Berliner Kindl Jubiläums Pils** (5.1%), which BKS assures us is different from and slightly more robust than their straight-up Pils, though the difference is subtle. This is a well-balanced, standard pilsner, deeper golden than most and with a little more bitterness.

Bottles include Hefeweissen beers from Erdinger, Berliner Weisse and Diebels Alt, a Düsseldorf altbier, brewed as a dark amber, malty ale to a recipe similar to a pre-war northern English bitter.

They have a sister pub, the Fulchen Hoppe, two doors down at Rathaus Straße 25.

53 **zum Nußbaum**
Am Nußbaum 3, 10178 Berlin-Mitte
T 030 242 3095
Good local food
U U2 (Klosterstraße)
S S3, S5, S7 & S75 (Alexanderplatz)
H M4, M5 & M6 (Spandauer Straße/Marienkirche)
Daily 12.00–02.00 (sometimes earlier)

The 'Nut Tree', in the heart of the restored Nikolaiviertel, is another Berlin institution; a dark, cosy, low-ceilinged and wood-panelled pub with a lovely little beer garden at the front – complete with nut tree of course. If Georgbræu (above) next door is too noisy and chaotic, seek refuge here and lunch in relative peace and quiet.

It has a tenuous claim to be the oldest pub in Berlin but as the original was in the Alt Colln area just across the River Spree and was destroyed in an air raid in 1943 we are not sure it qualifies.

That said, the replacement was rebuilt faithfully to the original design on the new site in 1986. A commemorative plaque in the bar pays tribute to its predecessor. There are three tiny rooms, each accommodating barely a dozen people.

By 2013 it should find itself just fifty metres from a new station on the extension to the U5 underground line.

The beer range is confined to the products of the Radeberger Gruppe, including Berliner Kindl Jubiläums Pils, Schöfferhofen Hefeweisse Hell and Märkisches Landmann Schwarz.
Our choice is **Potsdamer Rex Pils** (4.6%), originally from Potsdam would you believe? This light, straw-golden lager starts watery but has a smooth malt flavour and a bitter finish.

54 **Oberbaumeck (O.B.E.)**
Bevern Straße 5, 10997 Berlin-Kreuzberg
T 030 611 1617
www.oberbaumeck.com
None
U U1 (Schlesisches Tor)
Daily 17.00 till late

A taste of lively Hamburg, this is a shrine to the St Pauli football team and their skull & crossbones badge; punk music; and Hamburg beer.

This part of Kreuzberg was surrounded by the Wall on three sides and was traditionally the most anarchic and multi-ethnic part of West Berlin. It still is, though both elements rub along well together here. Back in those days the U1 line terminated here though it now extends over the river into the now fashionable Friedrichshain district of East Berlin. Gentrification here has been slower to take off.

O.B.E. is not designed for comfort. The seating looks like it came from a clearance sale, in contrast to the classic bar shelving and the huge photo of the Schlesisches Tor U-Bahn station in 1910 that covers the back wall.

St Pauli and HSV Hamburg games are shown live in preference to anything else but be warned, while this is a pretty easy-going joint, do not under any circumstances cheer for the latter.

The old St Pauli Brauerei in Hamburg was bought and closed by Holsten a decade ago. Its **Astra Pils** (4.8%), a light golden pilsner with full flavour and characteristic North German bitterness, is now brewed by Holsten themselves.

There are five draughts and eight bottles in all. The other draughts include Lübzer Pils from Mecklenburg, which borders Hamburg. The bottles include several Hefeweissen options, plus the excellent Köstritzer Schwarzbier.

55 zum Paddenwirt

55 **zum Paddenwirt** ⊗ ❄
Nikolaikirchplatz 6, 10178 Berlin-Mitte
T 030 242 6382
www.paddenwirt.de
🍴 Berlin specials, with vegetarian options
U U2 (Klosterstraße)
S S3, S5, S7 & S75 (Alexanderplatz)
BUS M45 (Mühlendamm/Nikolaiviertel)
🕐 Daily 12.00 till late

Right in the heart of Berlin, by the nave of the beautifully restored Nikolaikirche is this real local's pub in Black Forest scrubbed pine. Despite its central location, tourists rarely venture in. All the more reason for you to do so.

The 'Frog Landlord' takes its name from the story of a tavern on this site over 200 years ago, to which beer barrels were delivered by barge along the River Spree. One day, some barrels burst on the quayside and hundreds of frogs (*padden* in Berlin dialect) suddenly appeared, to drink the spillage. Once inebriated several of the frogs started to explode, providing the landlord (*wirt* in German) with an anecdote he told customers for decades to come. And the frog-motive still features throughout this distinctive and idiosyncratic little tavern.

The draught beers include Eibauer Pils, an easy-drinking but slightly metallic lager from the Münchbräu brewery in Sachsen (Saxony); Eibauer Schwarzbier; Schneider Weisse Hell; and Berliner Pils. There is also **Früh Kölsch** (4.8%), another of Cologne's finest, straw-lemon coloured, fresh, light and fruity, served in a straight-sided 20cl glass. Judge the quality by how long the *schaum* (head) lasts. Ten minutes is good, though whether you can nurse it for that long is doubtful.

Paulaner's im Spreebogen

56 Paulaner's im Spreebogen ✖ ✳

Alt Moabit 98, 10559 Berlin-Tiergarten

T 030 399 4332

www.paulaners-berlin.de

🍴 Bavarian

Ⓤ U9 (Turmstraße)

Ⓢ S3, S5, S7 & S75 (Bellevue)

🕐 Mo–Sa 11.00–24.00; Su 11.00–23.00

Berlin's first Bavarian-style beer hall is in a converted dairy between Alt Moabit and the river Spree. They really push the boat out, sparing no expense to recreate the magic of a night out in Munich.

Despite its size it is hard to find. From the U-Bahnhof head down Strom Straße. When you reach Zur Quelle (below), turn left into Alt Moabit. About 200m down, just after passing a gymnasium, turn right into a cobbled alley and the Paulaner's back entrance should be on your left.

We believe this was a brewpub for a time but proved too far off the beaten track to make brewing worthwhile. Things are different now, with several huge office developments along the River Spree boosting trade enormously, though the beer comes in from Munich.

Wednesday is Schweinhaxe day, meaning that gigantic oversized pork knuckle joints are served, balanced on a mountain of sauerkraut and potato dumplings, served with the health-enhancing addition of a tiny sliver of orange.

The full range of Paulaner beers are served, including Premium Pils, Original Munchener Dunkel, Hefeweiss Hell and arguably the best, **Paulaner Original Munchener Hell** (4.9%), served in a litre Maß of course. This is a classic Munich quaffing lager, malty and nutty with mineral notes and restrained hop bitterness.

57 Prater Garten & Gaststätte

57 Prater Garten & Gaststätte
Kastanienallee 7–9, 10435 Berlin-Prenzlauerberg
T 030 448 5688
www.pratergarten.de
🍽 Gastätte: full menu; Beer Garden: hearty snacks
Ⓤ U2 (Eberswalde Straße)
Ⓗ M1 & 12 (Eberswalder Straße/Danziger Straße)
🍺 Beer Garden: Daily from 12.00 (summer or fine weather only)
Gaststatte: Mo–Fr 18.00–24.00; Sa–Su 12.00–24.00

This pleasant, inexpensive retreat from the bustle of Prenzlauerberg, was formerly a cultural centre in the days of the DDR, featuring a dance hall, theatre and beer garden. It shut down soon after the Wall came down and state support ended, but re-opened as pub and beer garden in 1996.

The pub, or *Gaststätte*, has even more of a typical Bavarian beer hall feel here, probably because in contrast to Paulaner (above), all expense was spared in its furnishing and décor.

The beer garden seats over 600 and is the oldest in Berlin, dating from 1837. It comes with all the traditional trimmings – long tables and benches, plus horse chestnut trees with large clusters of leaves providing perfect shade.

The Prater has two special house beers, brewed we think by Frankfurter Bräuhaus in Frankfurt-Oder, 80km east of here, on the border with Poland. Prater Pils is a classic DDR-style swilling lager, the like of which has virtually disappeared – pleasant, moreish and malty sweet with little hop character.

The beer we recommend, for reasons of pure nostalgia, is the second of the house beers, **Prater Lager Schwarz** (5%). This black lager has a roasty aroma and big chocolate taste, is remarkably robust with a huge mouth feel and dry bitterness in the finish. It is served too cold but improves on warming.

The Gastätte also has Jever Pils on draught, whilst the beer garden has Weihenstephan Hefeweisse Hell.

Quell Eck

58 **Quell Eck**
Chaussee Straße 12, 10115 Berlin-Mitte
T 030 282 7868

Snacks only

U U6 (Oranienburger Tor)

Daily 12.00–02.00

Whether the character of this very basic local just north of the centre survives the double onslaught of popularity spreading from the south, and the huge office complexes being constructed from the north, remains to be seen.

Much of the latter will be a new HQ for the German intelligence agency, the Bundesnachtrichtendienst, which is relocating here from Munich. Its opening should improve the volume of custom but we hope will not temper the entertaining banter.

The bar is wonderfully obliterated with kitsch and boasts the oldest operational beer fount in Germany, dating from 1912. It also features a padded leather elbow rest along its length.

We have commented elsewhere about obscure sports featuring on German TV. It was here on our last visit that we watched international wheelchair fencing between France and Hong Kong. [When we left, France had a narrow lead.]

The draught beers here are Warsteiner Pils, Köstritzer Schwarzbier and the classic North German lager, **Jever Pils** (4.8%). Devastatingly dry and bitter with a green grass and parsley herb flavour, it was originally from a small regional brewery in the town of Jever, near Wilhelmshaven in German Friesland. Once a world classic, it has lost some edge since mass production followed multiple takeovers in the past two decades. Now made by the Radeberger Gruppe, it remains a fine beer.

59 zur Quelle
Alt-Moabit 87, 10559 Berlin-Tiergarten
T 030 391 4289
www.goerreseck.de
Breakfast, basic snacks
U U9 (Turmstraße)
24 hours a day

Zur Quelle is another basic corner local that somehow escaped the attention of both Bomber Command and the West Berlin planning authorities.

This is a *raucher lokal* (smoker's local) with chatty characters at the bar always ready with an opinion or two.

Open all hours, it makes an effort to keep its clientele with a steady stream of bingo evenings, special grill evenings, and a breakfast service. Besides this, food is limited to basic Bock or Knacker Wurst with a bit of stale bread.

Situated in a prominent location at the southeast corner of Alt Moabit and Strom Straße, it has a large pool room at the rear and a smaller front bar with a TV showing football games, especially those featuring local heroes Hertha BSC. Any goal scored by them during any match shown earns a free schnapps for everyone in the pub. That is how rarely they score.

The draught beers include the Berlin staples of Schultheiss Berliner Kindl Pils, the grittier Jever Pils, and **Erdinger Weißbier Hell** (5.3%), a yeasty, hazy beer with a banana aroma and a bitter citric finish. There is far less carbonation than is usual for a draught Hefeweisse, possibly because it is poured slowly and carefully here. We like it better that way.

Erdinger Weißbier Dunkel and Berliner Weisse feature amongst the bottled choices.

60 Restauration zur Gardestube 🏠 ❌
Rosen Straße 3, 12555 Berlin-Köpenick
T 030 6416 7431
🍴 Classic Berlin
Ⓢ S47 (Spindlersfeld, 1km) or S8, S9, S45 (Mo–Fr only) (Adlershof, 2km)
Ⓗ 60 or 61 from either S-Bahn
⊗ Sunday
🕐 Mo–Sa 10.00 till late

OK, let's get a few details clear. Avoid Köpenick S-Bahnhof because few of the many dozens of buses and trams that pass it head in the right direction. Instead take the S-Bahn to Adlershof and either tram line to Schlossplatz. From here turn the corner into Alt Köpenick, and Rosen Straße is first on your right, after the Rathaus – where the return tram stops.

That may seem like a lot of effort but the difficult journey pays dividends in the form of a fantastic time-warped backstreet local with a military theme that includes a life-sized guardsman mannequin inside his box. The pissed-up soldier sitting astride a rifle in the front window is another nice touch.

Of the four draughts, our choice is the much-mentioned **Köstritzer Schwarzbier** (4.8%), a dry and coffee-roast dark lager with a bitter finish. Many of these 'black beers' that now proliferate around the city are ultra-sweet concoctions but this is much better and thankfully, widely available.

The other draught choices are all pilsners, including Jarosover (from the Czech Republic), while there are also four bottled Hefeweissens. Beware the Rizdorfer Faßbrause though. It is a lemonade spritzer that some Berliners like to mix with their beer – quite why we are not sure.

61 **Reuterstuben**
Weser Straße 6, 12047 Berlin-Neukölln
T 030 6273 2883
www.reuterstuben.de
Snacks only, occasional breakfasts
U U7 & U8 (Hermannsplatz)
Daily 12.00 till late

Just off Hermannplatz, this gritty little pub is a handmade creation featuring two bars in one. The second is a nostalgia trip formed by the installation of features from a deceased nearby café where landlady Renata used to work. The impressive array of single-malt whiskies are also no more, alas – all the bottles are empty.

The huge Texas road scene mural in the billiards room at the back was painted by a friend who lived in the state for many years. Darts and *Skat* (a popular German card game, a bit like simplified bridge) are also played there, less easily when football is being shown on the TV.

On the first Sunday of every month, it is not unusual to see groups of elderly ladies tucking into – and usually finishing – vast plates of smoked salmon, cheese, ham, sausage, salad, fruit, peppered eggs, bread rolls, bratwurst, blutwurst, salami, pâtés and so on. This is the pub's gargantuan brunch, served from 09.00 to pre-booked groups only.

A couple of the beers are hand-picked too, including the rare **Schoppe Brau Helles** (5%), from the Südstern Brewpub (below), a spicy, big-flavoured unfiltered beer in which low carbonation increases drinkability and a slight mineral edge enhances the taste.

Among the bottled choices is another rarity, for Berlin at least, Licher Pils from Hessen. The schnapps list is good too.

62 Schalander

Bänsch Straße 91, 10247 Berlin-Friedrichshain
T 030 8961 7073
www.schalander-berlin.de

Interesting, high quality menu
U5 (Frankfurter Allee)
S8, S9, S41 & S42 (Frankfurter Allee)
Mo–Fr 15.00–01.00; Sa–Su 12.00–01.00

The Schalander is a cool, bright, open and uncluttered new brewpub on the corner of Bänsch Straße and Pettenkofer Straße in the eastern suburbs. Its well-crafted, unfiltered yet clear beers make it a welcome addition to the Berlin beer scene.

The 1.5 hectolitre brewing kit is displayed prominently behind a bar, the minimalist style of which allows just a few well-chosen prints of old Berlin.

There is a pleasant outdoor pavement terrace at the front and a separate smoking area inside, to the rear of the main bar.

The menu changes weekly, with chalkboard specials, and has a distinct southwest German (Baden) character though Flammkuchen from Alsace and Sunday roasts from the UK are there too.

The three draught Brauart beers include a reddish-amber Dunkel, biscuity with a slightly tart crab apple finish, which tastes too thin when served cold but fills out once the beer has warmed up a bit. The fresh and yeasty Weisse is dry, also with apple flavour. Our pick is the **Brauart Pilsner** (5%), a light, straw-coloured lager that tastes very fresh and quite bitter, but stays balanced by a biscuity malt base and has a grapefruit finish.

63 Schillerklause 🍺 ✕ €
Am Schillertheater 1, 10625 Berlin-Charlottenburg
T 030 313 5996
www.schillerklause.de
🍴 Snacks; all-you-can-eat 'Old Berlin Buffet' (from 17.00)
Ⓤ U2 (Ernst Reuter Platz)
🕐 Daily 15.00 till late

This snug little actors' bar next door to the Schiller Theatre has all the dramatic memorabilia one would expect, though the pool room at the back is a bit of a surprise. The excellent value Old Berlin Buffet is worth potting too.

The bar area allows smokers and sports a wonderful painted mural depicting the beer-fuelled chaos of a major backstage scene change between plays. Another cartoon, probably a self-parody by one of the actors, depicts a rotund gentleman in evening dress announcing that: "Whenever I go anywhere, my belly arrives before I do!"

To get here, follow the Schiller Straße signs in the U-Bahnhof and turn right down the street itself when you emerge. Am Schillertheater is the first on the right, after 150m.

There are three sound pilsners – Schultheiss, König and Jever – plus **Franziskaner Hefeweisse Hell** (5%), a refreshing, partially filtered Bavarian Weisse with so much banana from fermentation that the aroma follows through into almost a banana milkshake flavour.

The seven bottled beers include the same brewery's Weisse Dunkel.

Schlossplatzbrauerei

Schlossplatzbrauerei
Am Schlossplatz, 12555 Berlin-Köpenick
T 0176 2439 9568
www.schlossplatzbrauerei.de
None
S47 (Spindlersfeld, 1km) or S8, S9, S45 (Mo–Fr only) (Adlershof, 2km)
60 or 61 from either S-Bahn stop
Daily 12.00–23.00

Is this the smallest pub in Berlin? It claims to be, though we would not like to judge between here and the Alte Kolkshenke (above). Neither seats more than 30, and even that would be a crush, though there is some outside seating in summer.

The 'Castle Square Brewery' is a tiny, glass-sided brewpub. Utterly unique and quite charming, it is well worth the long journey from downtown, especially as you can combine a trip here with the equally alluring Restauration zur Gardestube (above) around the corner – the complex travel arrangements for which apply here as well.

The district of Köpenick was East Berlin's answer to Wannsee in the West, an attractive small town within the city limits surrounded by forests and lakes.

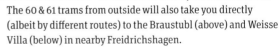

The 60 & 61 trams from outside will also take you directly (albeit by different routes) to the Braustubl (above) and Weisse Villa (below) in nearby Freidrichshagen.

There are two regular house beers. The lemony, hazy and tart Helles appears to have something of the wild yeast about it. Meanwhile, **Schlossplatzbrauerei Kupfer** (5.3%) is a deep brown beer with a robust coffee aroma, a malty and slightly sweet, coffee taste, finishing with some bitterness and liquorice. Not beautiful but certainly robust and interesting.

The seasonal Bock beers, when available, are pretty special too. On our last visit, this was an amber-coloured and quite potent beer, malty sweet, but with a hop balance to match.

65 Schmitz Katze

65 Schmitz Katze
Oranien Straße 163, 10969 Berlin-Kreuzberg
T 030 7071 5042
Snacks only
U U8 (Moritzplatz)
Daily 15.00–03.00

The name of this bar translates literally as "really quick cats" but a better colloquial translation would be moving like "a bat out of hell". A term applied to Michael Schumacher in his prime, we believe.

This bustling bar with a young clientele is in fashionable Oranien Straße, next door to Max und Moritz (above). Apart from the odd bit of post-modern artwork it is bare, open plan, smoker-friendly and loud, though come in the afternoon and it can be quiet and even deserted. This would be a good time to try the genuine UK dart board, not an electronic machine as in most German pubs. There is also a billiard table at the back.

Run by a Ukrainian lady called Tatiana Kourilskaia. Her personal taste is reflected in the "Where the f**k is Kyrgyzstan?" sticker behind the bar. Next to it is one featuring a large pig saying: "My meat belongs to me!", sat next to the crisps, nuts and Wiener sausages.

The four draught beers are Duckstein Schwarzbier (better than its reddish version), Berliner and Jever Pils and **Rothaus Tannenzäpfle** (5.1%), a very sharp, dry, fresh and bitter pilsner from the Black Forest in Baden Württemberg, southwest Germany.

The bottled range is good as well, including Astra Urtyp, a light-coloured Bock called Rothaus Eiszäpfle, three different Schneider wheat beers and the ubiquitous Berliner Weisse.

Schnelle Quelle

66 Schnelle Quelle
Rosa Luxemburg Straße 5, 10178 Berlin-Mitte
T 030 2809 6955
None
U U2, U5 & U8 (Alexanderplatz)
S S3, S5, S7 & S75 (Alexanderplatz)
Daily 15.00 till late

Dark, arty, cluttered and atmospheric, this bar for unreconstructed smokers attracts a great deal of passing tourist trade.

A piano perches on a balcony between the main bar and a mysterious back room that looks as if it might double as a small film studio. The bar is full of old maps and photos of Berlin, including one fascinating pictorial map from 1928 showing how tightly packed the buildings in the centre were before 1939–45 forced a radical redesign.

On the toilet doors are pictures of the ill-fated founders of the German Communist party. Karl Liebknecht is happily relieving himself, whereas Rosa Luxemburg's voluminous skirts precludes her from doing likewise.

During the afternoon, the TV screens show music videos from the 1980s and arthouse films, though the Bundesliga takes over at weekends, when the pub becomes the city centre's top venue for the sort of sports fans who like a drink and a smoke while others do the hard bit.

There are just three draught beers here: Berliner Pils, sickly-sweet Czech Krusovice Dark, and **Radeberger Pils** (4.8%), a sweetish, smooth and golden pilsner that is good without being special. Here they pour this beer correctly, which is to say slowly, giving it a pleasantly less obvious carbonation.

zum Schusterjungen

⑥⑦ **zum Schusterjungen** 🍺 ✖ 🍴
Danziger Straße 9, 10435 Berlin-Prenzlauerberg
T 030 442 7654
🍴 Good-value full menu
Ⓤ U2 (Eberswalderstraße)
Ⓗ M1, M10 & 12 (Danziger Straße/Schönhauser Allee)
🕐 Daily 11.00–24.00

The 'Cobblers Apprentice' was a famous Communist pub in the 1920s and early 30s, and was notorious for the pitched battles fought against the Nazi supporters who used the pub opposite – now a brunch venue called the Malzcafe.

It still retains much of its character from its DDR days, making it a lovely, unspoilt East Berlin local serving some of the best value pub grub in the city.

The front bar is clean and simple, with a wood carving of the eponymous apprentice strutting along a Berlin street, a newly made pair of boots slung over his shoulder. The rear part is the restaurant, although as in most places you can drink in the restaurant and eat in the bar.

Combine a visit here with a trip to the nearby Prater Garden (above). The Currywurst stall known as Konnopke's, underneath the railway arch by the U-Bahnhof, is said to the best in Berlin, as attested to by the huge queue than constantly snakes back from it.

Draught beers include Schultheiss, Märkishes Landmann Schwartz, Wernesgrüner Pils and our choice of **Berliner Bürgerbräu Pils** (5%), one of the very best from BKS. This beer has a slightly darker golden hue than most pilsners with a rounded, balanced taste and lovely bitter tang in the finish.

There are also three Hefeweissen from Erdinger (Hell, Dunkel & Kristall) plus Berliner Weisse.

68 Schwarzwaldstuben
Tucholsky Straße 48, 10117 Berlin-Mitte
T 030 2809 8084
www.scwarzwaldstuben-berlin.de
Breakfast from 09.00; full menu with Black Forest specialities from 11.00
U6 (Oranienburger Tor)
S1, S2 & S25 (Oranienburger Straße)
Daily 09.00–24.00

The 'Black Forest Pub' is on the corner of Tucholsky Straße and Linien Straße, the latter named because it followed the line of the old city walls, which were demolished in 1865. Come here for a taste of the Forest in beer and excellent food.

It is a magnet for the young, affluent, artistic crowd that has colonised most of the old working-class tenements in this part of town. It is surprising to see how many of these buildings survived wartime destruction.

The single long and spacious bar is littered with hunting trophies, including an enormous stuffed boar's head that sits a little uncomfortably with its cosmopolitan clientele. A raised seating area by the far window features plush sofas and chairs in pre-revolution French style.

The draught beers vary from month to month but always include Hefeweisse Hell and Tannenzäpfle Pils from Rothaus, Augustiner Helles and **Haller Löwenbrau Edel Pils** (4.9%), a dangerously quaffable, light straw-coloured lager from the Black Forest, nicely balanced by a citric bitterness more common in North German pilsners.

An above-average bottled selection includes Rothaus Eiszäpfle, Schwarzer Löwe, Augustiner Edelstoff and the rare and excellent Unertl Hefeweisse Dunkel. Service can be relaxed, but the excellence of the beer more than compensates.

69 Sophie'n Eck 🍺 ✗

Große Hamburger Straße 37, 10115 Berlin-Mitte

T 030 283 4065

www.sophieneck-berlin.de

🍽 Full menu

Ⓤ U8 (Weinmeisterstraße)

Ⓢ S3, S5, S7 & S75 (Hackesher Markt)

Ⓗ M1 & M6 (Monbijouplatz)

🕐 Daily 12.00–02.00

Clearly the DDR regime in its dying days had some junior cadre in the city planning department with a bit of foresight, as this place underwent a fabulous restoration in 1986, shortly before the Wall came down.

Dark and atmospheric, it features old oak, Persian rugs and interesting old prints in abundance. Although food-focused, there are plenty of stools around the small bar where one can simply sup a beer.

It began life in 1924, sharing the premises with a bakery and undertakers. Now in the heart of a rapidly gentrifying area just to the north of Hackesher Markt, full of fashion shops and smart restaurants, the Sophie'n Eck – named because it is on the corner of Sophien Straße – would be considered up-market by some. It is certainly popular. In good weather try to get a seat outside as this is a perfect location for people-watching.

The excellent food menu has vegetarian options and local specialities, including game in season.

The above-average draught beer range includes Jever Pils, Berliner Pilsner, Sion Kölsch and **Schlösser Alt** (4.8%), a classic light brown Düsseldorf altbier, fresh and smooth with slight roast and caramel notes, and some bitterness in the finish.

As well as Berliner Weisse the bottled range includes, rare-for-Berlin Störtebecker Schwarzbier, and four varieties of Schöfferhofer Hefeweizen.

Just around the corner at Krausnick Strasse 11 is 'Anna Koschke',
a delightful little cellar pub featuring good food and, inter alia, Jever Pils.

Strassenbahn

70 Strassenbahn
Laubacher Straße 29, 14197 Berlin-Wilmersdorf
T 030 821 7629
www.strassenbahn-kneipe.com
Extensive menu
U9 (Bundesplatz)
S41, S42 & S45 (Mo–Fr only) (Bundesplatz)
101 (Laubacher Straße/Varziner Straße)
Daily 16.00 till late

The 'Tram' (more literally 'Streetcar') is a characterful local almost next door to Hell oder Dunkel (above). Lucky locals.

It is the sole survivor of a six-strong pub collective started in 1977. The main bar is dominated by a huge photo of busy downtown Leipziger Straße circa 1920, and is often packed.

There is also a small smoking bar just off the main area, and a pleasant little beer garden along the side, parallel to the motorway.

All tips here go to charity, a sign behind the bar revealing that €6,000 had been disbursed to a number of good causes "recently", the biggest recipient being an Art Centre in Burkina Faso.

An extensive menu features cartoons extolling the consumption of beer and poking fun at fashion followers, vegetarians and – for some unexplained reasons – the Scots. Maybe they don't tip?

The beer selection is strong, with eight draughts and seven bottles. The former includes Lausitzer Bergquell, Wernesgrüner and König Pils, Duckstein, Memminger Hefeweizen Hell, Kloster Andechser Spezial Hell and **Gessner Alt-Sumbarcher Dunkel** (5.2%), a deep, ruby-brown stout-like lager from Thüringen, dry and smooth with a chocolate aroma, and strong roast coffee flavour.

The bottles are mainly wheat beers. The wine, spirits, cocktails and schnapps lists are equally robust.

71 Südstern

71 Südstern

Hasenheide 69, 10967 Berlin-Kreuzberg

T 030 69 001624

www.brauhaus-suedstern.de

Full menu

U U7 (Südstern)

Summer: Mo–Sa 14.00 till late; Su from 10.00
Winter: Mo–Fr 17.00 till late; Sa from 14.00; Su from 10.00

Formerly the 'Brauhaus Braams' and now the 'South Star', this large, open-plan brewpub is on a main road just north of Tempelhof airport. There is a small beer garden at the front, while a larger garden to the rear backs straight onto forest on the Hasenheide, or 'Rabbit Heath'.

It can be dauntingly quiet here during the day and they often host music, beer and culinary events in the evening to boost trade. The fabulous 'all-you-can-eat' Sunday brunch is worth the journey. Indeed all the food here is good, with both Berlin and Bavarian specialities served all day.

The on-site brewery also sells its wares to a few other places around Kreuzberg, often under different names from the Brauhaus Stern used here. For example, the excellent Heller becomes both Schöppe Brau (as at the Reuterstuben, above) and Kreuzberger Molle elsewhere. We have no idea why.

The other regular draughts, all unfiltered, are the Weisse, with an unusual chocolaty aroma and dry, nutty taste; and **Brauhaus Dunkler Stern** (5.2%), a ruby-brown beer that somehow weaves together quite successfully chocolate cake aromas and flavours with elderflower bitterness to make a great quaffing beer despite its intensity.

On our last visit there was also a seasonal Bok on tap, strong (6.7%), blonde, yeasty and nutty, with some pepper spice and a flowery finish.

Thüringer Stuben

72 Thüringer Stuben
Stargarder Straße 28, 10437 Berlin-Prenzlauerberg
T 030 446 3339
www.thueringer-stuben.de
Thüringen specialities
S8, S9, S41 & S42 (Prenzlauer Allee)
M2 (Fröbel Straße)
Mo–Sa 16.00 till late; Su 12.00 till late

It may be a little folksy or homely, even kitsch, with fairy lights twinkling all year round, cuckoo clocks in abundance and hunting accoutrements springing from every available corner, but boy, is this tavern popular. We have rarely found it anything other than full.

On the corner of Duncker Straße, this little slice of Thüringen, complete with state flag, serves up first class food, with *wild* (game) specialities such as deer, venison, boar and duck, good local Thüringian wine and *Äpfelstrudel* all to the fore.

There is no beer garden or separate smoking bar, so this is a rare case of a Berlin pub where smokers, even in winter, must stand on the pavement braving the elements, as they do elsewhere in Europe.

It also offers several beers that we have not spotted anywhere else in Berlin. Included in the draught beers are three from Thüringen. Apoldaer Pils is tasty and bitter, if a little thin; Apoldaer Hefeweisse is a fairly standard Weisse lacking a bit of bite; and **Meininger Pils** (5%), a golden-coloured, crisp and lemony pilsner with a creamy, off-dry texture and a bitter finish.

The bottled beers are unexceptional.

97

Tiergartenquelle

73 Tiergartenquelle
Bach Straße 6, S-Bahnbogen 482, 10555 Berlin-Tiergarten
T 030 392 7615
www.tiergartenquelle.de
German, hearty portions
U U9 (Hansaplatz)
S S3, S5, S7, S75 (Tiergarten)
Mo–Fr 17.00–24.00; Sa–Su 12.00–01.00

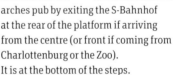

You can stagger straight off the S-Bahn platforms down into this atmospheric, underneath-the-arches pub by exiting the S-Bahnhof at the rear of the platform if arriving from the centre (or front if coming from Charlottenburg or the Zoo).
It is at the bottom of the steps.

This is really two pubs merged into one, the more northerly being an overspill bar. Both are cluttered with bric-a-brac and posters advertising theatre and music events. The overspill has sofas. In winter, smokers must retreat to a diddy windowless room at the back, where a real fug soon develops. In summer, the beer garden would be a better choice.

As the name suggests, this spot is handy for the Tiergarden, Berlin's answer to London's Hyde Park.

The food is excellent and comes in enormous portions. Vegetarians will typically have a choice of seven main course options, while carnivores get a whole page on steaks alone.

This pub is owned by Lemke and is a welcome extra outlet for their wares. These include their Hefeweisse and whatever seasonal creation happens to be on, plus **Brauhaus Lemke Pils** (5%), filtered specially for here. Counterintuitively, it tastes better this

way, flowering as a crystal clear, deep-gold pilsner, lemony and full-bodied with a bitter-sweet finish. We suggest you try both versions and make your own mind up.

All beers are available in litre Maß jugs if you wish.

Vogt's Bier Express

 Vogt's Bier Express 🍺
Mehringdamm 32/34, 10961 Berlin-Kreutzberg
T 030 251 2529
E info@vogts-bierexpress.de
🍴 No Food
Ⓤ U6 & U7 (Mehringdamm)
🕐 Mo–Fr 09.00–01.00; Sat & Sun 09.00–02.00

This pub is unique in this guide as being the only one that serves no food yet smoking is still *verboten*, at least in the main bar. A *Raucher-Lounge* is advertised, but we have yet to locate it. No matter, seating on the pavement caters for smokers whilst one can bring in any food one likes and eat it in the pub, which conveniently, is flanked by a curry-wurst shop on one side and a kebab stall on

the other. Judging from the ever-present, enormous (but fast-moving) queues, these fast-food joints must be amongst the best in all Berlin.

This is a really distinctive local drinking-den, strong on TV sport and choc full with bric-a-brac that is cool and kitsch in roughly equal measure. The 'box panorama' of the pub itself definitely belongs amongst the latter. But the 1930's direction sign to an airship landing field juxtaposed next to a fabulous DDR poster from the early 1950's, that features the flower of (East) German youth gazing in rapt adoration at a portrait of Joseph Stalin, are very much the former. The caption says, "Stalin – now that's freedom."

The beer! There are six draft taps featuring Berliner Kindl Jubiläums Pils, Bitburger Pils, Beck's, Duckstein and both the Helles and Original from Schneider Weiss, the famous wheat-beer brewery in Kelheim in Bavaria, whose brewery tap remains in Munich. Do not be put off by the muddy-brown complexion of **Schneider Weiss Original** (5.4%), for this is a superb example of the style; fresh with a big toffee and banana flavour balanced by restrained apple bitterness in the finish. Kindl Berliner Weisse and Diebels Alt are the only bottled offerings of note.

Weihenstephaner

75 Weihenstephaner ✪ ✪
Neue Promenade 5, Am Hackesher Markt, 10178 Berlin-Mitte
T 030 2576 2871
www.weihenstephaner-berlin.de
🍴 Bavarian
Ⓢ S3, S5, S7 & S75 (Hackesher Markt)
🕐 Daily 11.00–01.00

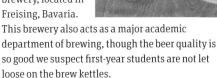

This is the chief Berlin outlet for Wiehenstephaner beers from the world's oldest brewery, located in Freising, Bavaria. This brewery also acts as a major academic department of brewing, though the beer quality is so good we suspect first-year students are not let loose on the brew kettles.

The pub is a small, up-market version of a Bavarian beer hall, with a smart restaurant area at the rear and expansive terrace on the busy square at the front. A more secluded beer garden is located at the back.

There is also a cellar bar downstairs that looks as though it really did store beer barrels at one time. The whole establishment exudes cool, with great food served from an extensive, Bavarian-themed menu. There is also a good schnapps collection and an excellent wine list.

All the draught beers are from the Weihenstephan brewery, and include Hefeweisse Hell, Hefeweisse Dunkel, Kristal Weisse, Original, Tradition Dunkel, Pils and Hefeweisse Light (for drivers), with monthly specials such as **Vitus** (7.7%), a meaty, blonde Weizenbock.

The only bottled beer regularly available is **Weihenstephan Korbinian** (7.4%), a glorious, dark, dry and strong Doppelbock with malt and chocolate flavours to the fore, and some dry fruit in the finish. This type of beer can be sickly sweet in Germany, but not this one. The beer menu describes it as 'elegant' and we agree.

76 Weisse Villa ✖ ❋
Josef-Nawrocki Straße 10, 12587 Berlin-Köpenick
T 030 6409 5646
www.weissevilla.com
Smart restaurant; menu also available in beer garden
S3 (Freidrichshagen)
Daily 11.00–24.00

It is stretching definitions to call the 'White Villa' a pub. Rather, it is a wonderful, palatial old house with touches of faded grandeur that houses a smart restaurant and (in summer only) a double-decker beer garden with magnificent views over the Müggelsee.

Both restaurant and garden serve the full range of Berliner Bürgerbräu (BBB) beers, as does the Bräustubl (above) next door. To get here, follow the instructions for the Bräustubl (above), then turn left into Müggelsee Damm and right almost immediately into Josef-Nawrocki Straße. Head into the courtyard of the old brewery and follow signs to the beer garden.

Alternatively, go straight though the main door and into the restaurant where, once installed, white-waistcoated waiters will pamper you and suggest you might order half a roast duck, the house speciality.

Brewing should soon restart inside the old BBB brewery, in a new microbrewery

producing beer under a new name – Köpenicker Brauerei. The original brewery and brands were bought by Radeberger Gruppe and currently everything is brewed at BKS, though the quality seems to have survived.

The beers available include BBB Pils, their copper-coloured lager called Rotkelchen, BBB Bernauer Schwarz, and **Berliner Bürgerbräu Weissbier** (5%), a soft, spicy, grainy, vanilla-banana brew with a hint of lingering citric tartness, brewed originally as a Berliner Weisse but moved on. Either way, perfect for a summer afternoon lazing by the lake.

Westend Klause

77 **Westend Klause**
Reichs Straße 80, 14052 Berlin-Charlottenburg
T 030 3032 8471
www.westend-klause.de
None
U U2 (Neu-Westend)
Mo–Fr 16.00–04.00; Sa 12.00–04.00; Su 14.00–04.00

Max Schmelling, who was world heavyweight boxing champion in 1930–32 was reportedly a regular at this lively local way out west, dating from 1920.

The sporting connections continue in that this is also the closest decent bar to the nearby Olympia Stadion, site of the infamous 1936 Berlin Olympics, restored and given a roof for the 2006 World Cup. The stadium is now the home of Hertha Berlin FC, and most of their games are shown on a big screen TV in the bar.

The pub is dark with wood panelling throughout, and a wooden floor. Look out for the frieze painted around the room, featuring boozing and dancing locals. This is made out of numerous panels, each depicting a humorous or risqué event, that were prepared annually for a now long-defunct local festival. Not quite the Parthenon perhaps, but still a nice touch. Also beware the vertiginous descent down to the toilets in the basement – designed as a feedback mechanism for drinkers who may have had one too many.

To get here from the U-Bahn take the eastern 'Reich Straße' exit rather than the one marked Olympia Stadion – unless you are planning on some tourism first. You can see the pub from the station exit.

The four draught beers here are Jever, Engelhardt and Berliner Pils, and **Schöfferhofer Hefeweizen Hell** (5%) from Frankfurt-am-Main, a lively, fruity and slightly sour beer. There are bottled wheat beers from Erdinger.

Willy Bresch

78 **Willy Bresch** 🏛 🚏
Danziger Straße 120, 10407 Berlin-Prenzlauerberg
T 030 425 0905
🍴 Snacks only
Ⓢ S8, S9, S41 & S42 (Greifswalder Straße)
Ⓗ M4 & M10 (Greifswalder Straße/Danziger Straße)
🕐 Hours unclear (we have never found it shut...!)

We have no idea who Willy Bresch is or was. He appears to have left no mark on the world except for the pub bearing his name, which is an absolute classic. An atmospheric, basic local that is, for what it's worth, the author's favourite bar in Berlin.

It is located on the southeast corner of the major road junction with Griefswalder Straße. On the way there from the S-Bahnhof in Greifswalder Straße, look out for the Soviet-style statue in homage to Ernst Thällman, leader of the Communist Party in the pre-Hitler Reichstag, in the park that bears his name.

Above the front door is a wonderful mural depicting old market traders selling flowers and fish. Inside are simple check tablecloths, a wooden floor, old photos of Berlin and a ceramic beer jug collection.

The shelving behind the bar promises an interesting schnapps experience, which the menu delivers in spades.

In addition to Berliner Pils and Schultheiss Pils, two excellent beers from the small Hohenthanner brewery in Bavaria are also served – at amazingly low prices. Hohenthanner Dunkel manages to be malty and bitter at the same time, while **Hohenthanner Tannen Pils** (5%), is a delightfully smooth and balanced lager, served here at a temperature that does not compromise its character.

Don't be surprised if the locals start dancing to classic German kitsch muzak, nor if they invite you to join in!

79 Yorckschlösschen
Yorck Straße 15, 10965 Berlin-Kreuzberg
T 030 215 8070
www.yorckschloesschen.de
Full menu from 12.00; breakfast from 10.00 (summer only)
U U6 & U7 (Mehringdamm)
Daily 10.00–03.00

On the corner of Grossbeeren Straße where Yorck Straße veers left, this Berlin institution offers live jazz and blues twice a week (Sunday afternoons 14.00–18.00, and Wednesday evenings from 21.00).

It opens up into room after room the deeper one penetrates the interior, though there is a shady beer garden out the front. Like many Berlin hostelries, the 'Schlösschen' is quiet and comfortable during the day, when Delta blues will likely be playing in the background. It livens up considerably at night, especially on Wednesdays. Photos of the jazz greats adorn the walls.

It is 120 years old and named after Prussian general, Yorck von Wartenburg, who rose to prominence during the Napoleonic Wars.

The snacks are large enough to pass for a full meal. If you go for the Leberkäse und Brotchen (for just €2,80), you are unlikely to need another even four hours later. If you are tiring of beer, the long schnapps list will see you right (or off, perhaps).

The draught beers are Veltins Pils, Jever Pils, Hohenthanner Tannen Pils, Gaffel Kölsch, Hohenthanner Hefeweisse, and **Hohenthanner Tannen Dunkel** (5.2%), arguably less satisfying than that brewery's pilsner (see previous entry), slightly thin and astringent to start, but with a dry, malty and burnt taste, and a touch of bitterness at the finish.

The bottled offerings include Neuzeller Klosterbräu and, of course, Berliner Weisse.

Zillemarkt

80 Zillemarkt
Bleibtreu Straße 48a, 10623 Berlin-Charlottenburg
T 030 881 7040
www.zillemarkt.de
Full menu
U U1 (Uhland Straße)
S S3, S5, S7 & S75 (Savigny Platz)
Mo–Fr 12.00–24.00; Sa–Su 10.00–24.00

This cavernous pub has strong hints of Art Deco, especially in its ceilings.

It is named after one Heinrich Ziller born in 1858, a famous and by all accounts larger-than-life cartoonist and caricaturist who pioneered 'gutter press' journalism in Berlin. His work, if it can be described as such, is preserved as prints and displayed here.

The pub itself has a long, high and much-stooled bar with a restaurant area to the rear. There is also a quiet, attractive and secluded beer garden. Look out for the British phone box.

The food menu is enormous and varied.

The pub and its bar staff have on occasion claimed that its 'house' beer is brewed on the premises but on our most recent visit admitted that it is brewed in a small private brewery some-

where in Brandenburg, though we know not where.

Either way, this house beer is called **Zillebräu** (5%) and is actually rather good, wherever it comes from. Light, unfiltered and straw-coloured beer, it is moreish with a pronounced citrus-bitter flavour.

The pub's other beers are more mainstream – Bitburger Pils, Berliner Pils, Weihenstephan Hefeweisse and Köstrizer Schwarzbier, with a few bottles including guess what?

Brewers and their beers

At the latest count Germany had around 1,375 operational breweries and rising.
For the only up-to-date English language guide to them all, we recommend you invest in
a copy of Steve Thomas's 2007 *Good Beer Guide Germany* and its 2011 supplement,
the latter only available from Cogan & Mater Ltd at **www.booksaboutbeer.com**.

Here we list only the beers that appear in our text, arranged region by region, brewery by brewery.

BERLIN

BKS (Radeberger Gruppe)
67 Berliner Bürgerbräu Pils (5%)
15 Berliner Bürgerbräu Rotkehlchen (5.3%)
76 Berliner Bürgerbräu Weissbier (5%)
1 Berliner Kindl Bock Dunkel (7%)
52 Berliner Kindl Jubiläums Pils (5.1%)
3 Berliner Kindl Pils (4.6%)
5 Berliner Kindl Weisse (3%)
39 Berliner Pils (5%)
25 Engelhardt Pils (5%)
53 Potsdamer Rex Pils (4.6%)
42 Schultheiss Pils (5%)

Brauhaus Bohnsdorf
11 Bohnsdorf Dunkel (5.8%)

Brauhaus Mitte
12 Brauhaus Mitte Hefeweisse Hell (5%)

Brauhaus in Spandau
33 Brauhaus Spandau Havelbräu Hell (5.2%)
14 Brauhaus Spandau Spezialbier (5.0–5.5%)

Brewbaker
16 Brewbaker Pils (5%)

Eschenbräu
23 Eschenbräu Pils (5%)

Georgbräu
28 Georg Pils (5%)

Hops & Barley
35 Hops & Barley Bio Pilsner (4.8%)

Lemkes Spezialitätenbrauerei/Lemke am Schloß
41 Brauhaus Lemke Original (5.5%)
40 Brauhaus Lemke Weisse (5%)
73 Brauhaus Lemke Pils (filtered) (5%)

Lindenbräu
44 Lindenbräu Hofbräu-Weiße (5%)

Marcus Bräu (Bräuhaus Alexanderplatz/Barkowsky)
45 Marcus Bräu Pils (5%)

Rollberg (former Kindl brewery)
37 Rollberg Hell (5%)

Schalander
62 Brauart Pilsner (5%)

Schlossplatzbrauerei
64 Schlossplatzbrauerei Kupfer (5.3%)

Südstern
71 Brauhaus Dunkler Stern (5.2%)
61 Schoppe Brau Helles (5%)

BADEN-WÜRTTEMBERG

Haller Löwenbrau *from Schwäbisch Hall*
68 Haller Löwenbrau Edel Pils (4.9%)

Rothaus *from Rothaus*
65 Rothaus Tannenzäpfle (5.1%)

BAVARIA (BAYERN)

Andechs *from Andechs*
50 Kloster Andechs Doppelbock Dunkel (7%)
26 Kloster Andechs Spezial Hell (5.8%)
17 Kloster Andechs Weissbier Hefetrub (5.5%)

Augustiner *from Munich*
2 Augustiner Edelstoff (5.6%)
19 Augustiner Helles (5.2%)
6 Augustiner Pils (5.6%)

Bayreuther *from Bayreuth*
8 Bayreuther Zwickl Kellerbier (5.3%)

Erdinger *from Erding*
10 Erdinger Weißbier Dunkel (5.6%)
59 Erdinger Weißbier Hell (5.3%)
48 Erdinger Kristall (5.3%)

Fürstlich Fürstenbergische Brauerei *from Donaueschingen*
24 Fürstenberg Pils (4.8%)

Heller *from Bamberg*
51 Aecht Schlenkerla Rauchbier Märzen (5.1%)

Hofbräuhaus Traunstein *from Traunstein*
34 Altbairisch Dunkel (5.3%)

Hohenthanner Schlossbrauerei *from Hohenthann*
79 Hohenthanner Tannen Dunkel (5.2%)
78 Hohenthanner Tannen Pils (5%)

Kulmbacher *from Kulmbach*
36 Kulmbacher Mönchshof Schwarzbier (4.9%)

Maisel *from Bayreuth*
32 Maisel's Weisse Original (5.2%)

Memminger *from Memmingen*
29 Memminger Pils (5.1%)

Paulaner *from Munich*
56 Paulaner Original Munchener Hell (4.9%)

Schneider *from Kelheim*
74 Schneider Weiss Original (5.4%)

Spaten-Franziskaner *from Munich*
63 Franziskaner Hefeweisse Hell (5%)

Streck-Bräu *from Ostheim vor der Rhön*
31 Streck's Pils (4.8%)

Weihenstephan *from Freising*
75 Weihenstephan Korbinian (7.4%)
46 Weihenstephaner Pils (5.1%)

Brewery unknown
21 Kiez Bier (5%)

BRANDENBURG

Frankfurter *from Frankfurt-am-Oder*
57 Prater Lager Schwarz (5%)

Klosterbrauerei Neuzelle *from Neuzelle*
9 Kyritzer Mord und Totschlag (7.2%)

Brewery unknown
13 Rixdorfer Hell (5.2%)
80 Zillebräu (5%)

HAMBURG

Holsten *from Hamburg-Altona*
54 Astra Pils (4.8%)

HESSEN

Binding-Henninger *from Frankfurt-am-Main*
77 Schöfferhofer Hefeweizen Hell (5%)

LOWER SAXONY (NIEDERSACHSEN)

Jever *from Jever*
58 Jever Pils (4.8%)

NORTH RHINE-WESTPHALIA (NORDRHEIN-WESTFALEN)

Barre *from Lübbecke*
47 Barre Bräu Pils (4.8%)

Erzquell *from Bielstein*
30 Bergisches Löwenpils (4.8%)

Früh *from Köln (Cologne)*
55 Früh Kölsch (4.8%)

Gaffel *from Köln (Cologne)*
49 Gaffel Kölsch (4.8%)

König *from Duisberg*
20 König Pils (4.9%)

Paderborner *from Paderborn*
38 Isenbeck Pils (4.8%)

Schlösser *from Düsseldorf*
69 Schlösser Alt (4.8%)

Warsteiner *from Warstein*
43 Warsteiner Premium Verum (4.8%)

RHINELAND-PALATINATE (RHEINLAND-PFALZ)

Bitburger Braugruppe GmbH *from Bitburg*
27 Bitburger Pils (4.8%)

SAXONY (SACHSEN)

Radeberger Exportbierbrauerei (Radeberger Gruppe) *from Radeberg*
66 Radeberger Pils (4.8%)

SCHLESWIG-HOLSTEIN

Flensburger *from Flensburg*
22 Flensburger Pils (4.9%)

THURINGIA (THÜRINGEN)

Gessner *from Sonneberg*
70 Gessner Alt-Sumbarcher Dunkel (5.2%)

Gotha *from Gotha*
18 Waidbauer Pils (4.7%)

Köstritzer *from Köstritz*
60 Köstritzer Schwarzbier (4.8%)

Meininger Privatbrauerei *from Meiningen*
4 Ambrosius Export (5.2%)
7 Ambrosius Pils (5%)
72 Meininger Pils (5%)

Berlin suburbs

See next spread for inset of city centre

TIERGARTEN

Zoologischer
Garten

CHARLOTTENBURG

SCHÖNEBERG

WILMERSDORF

TEMPLEHOF

0   1km

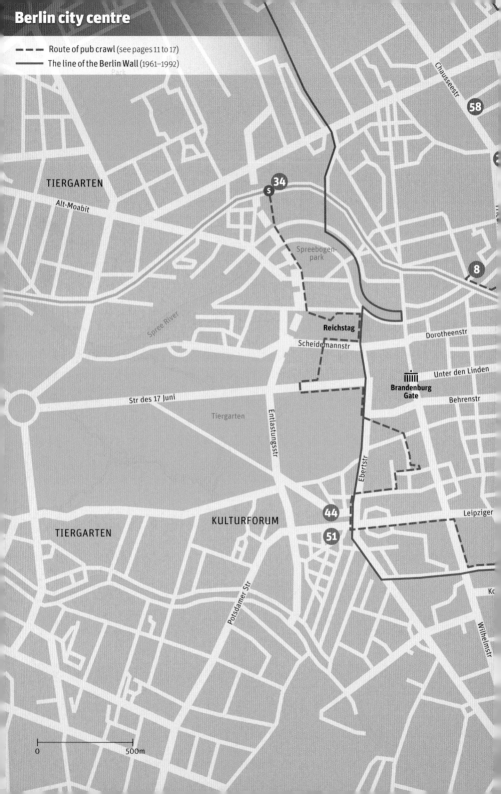

Berlin city centre

- - - Route of pub crawl (see pages 11 to 17)
───── The line of the Berlin Wall (1961–1992)

TIERGARTEN

Alt-Moabit

Park

S **34**

58

Spreebogen-park

8

Spree River

Reichstag

Scheidemannstr

Dorotheenstr

Unter den Linden

Brandenburg Gate

Behrenstr

Str des 17 Juni

Tiergarten

Entlastungsstr

Ebertstr

TIERGARTEN

KULTURFORUM

44

Leipziger

51

Potsdamer Str

Wilhelmstr

Ko

0   500m

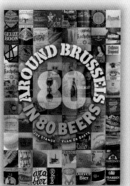